SELECTED POEMS

Gig Ryan was born in 1956 and grew up in Melbourne. Her first UK publication, *Selected Poems* (Bloodaxe Books, 2012), was published in Australia in 2011 by Giramondo under the title *New and Selected Poems*. She has published six other collections of poetry in Australia: *The Division of Anger* (1981); *Manners of an Astronaut* (1984); *The Last Interior* (1986); *Excavation* (1990); *Pure and Applied* (1998), which won the Victorian Premier's Award for Poetry (C.J. Dennis Prize); and *Heroic Money* (2001).

Ryan is also a freelance reviewer and a songwriter, performing and releasing three albums with Disband (1988) and Driving Past (1999, 2006). She lives in Melbourne, and has been poetry editor of the Melbourne *Age* since 1998.

GIG RYAN

SELECTED
POEMS

BLOODAXE BOOKS

ISBN: 978 1 85224 921 2

First published in the UK in 2012 by
Bloodaxe Books Ltd,
Highgreen,
Tarset,
Northumberland NE48 1RP.

www.bloodaxebooks.com
For further information about Bloodaxe titles
please visit our website or write to
the above address for a catalogue.

Supported by
**ARTS COUNCIL
ENGLAND**

First published in Australia by Giramondo Publishing
in 2011 as *New and Selected Poems*.

This project has been assisted by the Australian Government through
the Australia Council for the Arts, its arts funding and advisory body.

Australian Government | **Australia Council**
for the Arts

Cover design: Neil Astley & Pamela Robertson-Pearce.

Printed in Great Britain by
Bell & Bain Limited, Glasgow, Scotland.

CONTENTS

from **HEROIC MONEY** (2001)

The Division of Anger

(1981)

Cool Black August / Point Lonsdale

In a green house, insects bat the netted window
curtains coming gently forward then still, with proper gravity
The ocean unrolls like cloth into the shore

Trees rustle like a cough, the green house dims
amongst back-weeds, and a dog-chain sounds
through blue street mist

You climb into the dune, curved around the bay
like a castle wall, to feel less the moth
at windows, beating for a strange hand
to unwind a window sill

Tight air curls the open heart
now running down, slipped once, and racing
down, like a black wave, down, bones spray
the grey sand raw

A chair skids abruptly over floorboards,
scars onto a nail. The fireplace is whispering
Tired Peter loosens against cane
a limp page scatters

You will sleep in a green house
like weeds
The ocean tumbling like a child.

Stopwatch

I lived with a madman in a craven house
to sate me formless, tired of jutting like a broken rod,
to grow calm with anger

To let him snatch with teeth, and die
backyard heathens with a blown gate unlatched
and banging

His pale blue eyes at morning weeping slowly
like the sky, weeping, turn the face away
His pale tears down my back

For a clear afternoon,
when I would close a gate like that
and let his cold vein white on a hot day

I lived alone, discarding all the deaths sheeted
over eyes, washed by a thin man's voice
but went through yellow leaves

And those who wait like fishermen
perhaps will be repaired, not need to cross the tyrant's line
or listen to the pier shriek in places

My safety kicks out like a spring from a frugal chair
or a slither of child beneath stretched skin
and nothing will rub this soreness from my wrists, my bones

Getting It

1

This'll take the edge off it he says
with his warm tongue like the bastard
He is.
How 'bad' you felt the next night
with his friend. How green you are
worried like a kid, but there.

He kisses, his pale guilt blowing
like a flower. You're luxurious, unsure.
Your eyes opening like telescopes
on a clean brain.
You're so silly in the kitchen, like a new appliance.

At night the walls' pattern goes rash
and Didn't he notice then,
his eyes falling larger than a scream.
You could've been wrong. It happens.

———

Unintelligently, he's soft
by the economic fridge, his green eyes
green as crying, taking talk
between his serious hands, he spreads
it on the table like a telegram
that moans through wire.
You look out at the city
with your endless face shimmering in the window.

———

Will you buy me a dark salmon citroën
please, with all your brilliant money,
how it smells like a bank-clerk.

2

You're sitting there, argumentative as love, and callous.
Will your wisdom like an orange crane lift you silent?
The couples regret each other noisily.
A woman peers into your eyes, her children plugged
into the next room like a continent.
How she wants to talk to you, probing
the inexchangeable man between your thighs.
Irritable as weather across the table,
you remove yourself with something orthodox.

Across the wide car's seat, she's miles away.
Your head severe behind the dashboard, smoking.
He's in some pale yellow room,
the skirting-boards sealing like band-aids,
the nature strips outside.
He's passing regularly the unconditional rooms
where children squawk your name over
don't they, like a fable.

Big romance paddles the water
with sticky lights monitoring it down
between the seventh floor and the neon.
The rings of death are dribbling to the ocean,
papery and timid.
His environmental love, his city mouth,
hushed up like a tree.

Let me lie with you, your glamorous dreams,
in these clean and temporary sheets.
A car moans against the kerb
and steals me, as your suburb winds
the darkness.

The water lies down like a saint.
He sleeps like a dream.

Dying for It

1

Out that door when I leave I'll disintegrate
in your backyard / a medal to live there,
into my silent address, into the absolute realm
with this idiot love trembling like a car.

He says he needs a space for being.
My alien head rigs the coloured lights,
they infect the table we go down in like a pond.
When I can believe someone else I'll stop lying.

Into the taut blue bridge I was delivered
adrift the ceaseless water, blue as flowers,
pale blue like 'This *is* fun'
where dawn is white shock on the water.

He copes with the table.
I would kill a thousand crocodiles for you.
His sincerity clacking like chainmail,
death-hot, and your dead throat moves
one dream down.

2

Into the rupture of your blond thighs
our unease spills past recognition.

Into the colourless room, where night sets in like a slave.
Your black lung singing sleep.

You push your ocean through the needle.
How proud the city shifts the window.
My eyes, wide as an oven, still carol you.
All the vigorous dead come back. Remember. Remember.
Your voice drags like footsteps.

3

He hands you fun in a glass jar.
Back in Sydney, you discover the exclamation-mark,
pumping the beach-resort of his conversation.
You work hard to get them talking.
His American optimism sweet on the sky
she's going gaga over.

Your heroic gestures fall flat.
He becomes the transience of this hour, unscathed, cordial, and dying.
I've got to be hungry to get romantic.
And you're both crazy, theoretically, at last,
with that timid music rising like a mass
chanting Join hands and it'll all go away.

4

Now his voice compels you,
that futureless easy kiss, compels you outward.
Her sandy arms will wrap you
sympathetic above the longest table.
Forgive this damage, always.

5

I will go down into the black water
and peel its wetness back into the shore
where it will shiver like a dress.
Down between the dry rock and the soft weed
is this green blood drawn.
From the close dream and the indefinite past
the black sky calling birth.

Cruising

I dreamt I drank too much lemonade
and it was fatal. Everybody pointed and ran.
The man came into my room in his office clothes.
Go away I said, and I jumped out of my skin.

In the Italian café, I think of the wealthy.
What helicopter must have sunk into the roof
to be used so precariously by the management,
or contrived. (It's common *now*)
I stare at the propellor, it shudders like a failure.
Who can eat under that?

You can see from the street they've added another storey.
The pilot's capsule's been renovated, hired out
for secret occasions, furtive and giddy, so secret
we never heard. I'd find it claustrophobic
and ruin my clothes. (After the bill gets drenched,
the waiter takes it to dry in a microwave oven)
A friend told me it's been rigged without gravity,
looking red and expensive. His mouth sloped down,
about to reveal something xenophobic. I had to leave.

Is there a word which means 'fear of things falling on you'?
I wake up and look at the split in my ceiling.
I jump out of my skin again, glad that I smoke,
glad that I can become historical and calm at the same time,
thinking of how non-smokers taste when you kiss them,
pink and wet and physical like a baby.

Not Like a Wife

He questions her, his face soft with lovely money.
Be my mistress. He's French, polite as corruption.
Yes. Her clothes are dirty. Love has made me poor.
She leans against the flimsy cupboard, wrapping her face up
in her hands. I loved a rich man
once, but I was never blonde, and suntans you know,
so bland. I never looked American enough
on the beach.

I'll take you to Bangkok he says, the jewellery.
I can't wear it. The nightclubs. Yes.
You could look like a million dollars you know,
touching her shirt collar, if you had it.
I can't cook. His dark eyes soft and persistent
as flesh, wise with money he talks.
You like it here yes, you find character in poverty?
His arms snatch the whole creaking house up.
He's laughing at the plaster. You're so frank and evasive.
It's alright, really, tense as a movie,
watching carlights flash above the bed.
He loved me once. You're new, aren't you.

The sink's blocked in Darlinghurst.
I never could eat spaghetti effectively,
too unmarried or something.

How I Went

I'm wearing my mother's honeymoon shirt,
its softness thins in parts,
thinking of how I went for you,
total as a lunatic, my blue surgery hands
that will always allow you.

She looked prettier in it, better.
I make it hang like a desperate word.
Her eternal face I can't look at.
My love slides in your throat
without meaning.
I will give you quiet and sleep.

This love lifts me like a bright white star
but who can stand that?
I will stain it with skin and pale grey voices,
I'll land on it and poke it with a flagpole
until I fade into coherence,
sick at heart and no stranger.

Sunday

My father's grave face asks,
as the heart clicks over, covered,
about the man. I'm crying,

and won't resist, and not dutiful,
as the heart comes out
like a mouth, sure and unwilling.

and why I'm going so soon,
into the restless future. Break.

as he sees where my mouth has been
and what the skin's been cut on.
My mother in the kitchen calls him back,
showing, Talk to her.

as the coffin stirs in the back-seat,
taking the corner like a man.

My sister takes my head against her neck.

January

January is tearless as shampoo, entertaining and marketable.
She wraps her hair up, worthlessly.
While here, having survived Hiroshima, a cockroach sits,
smaller than a policeman's heart.
For the pain, she says, pointing at it,
as her limp eyes stare and wander,
scuffles the sheet under her chin, and worries like a tablet.

And that young man. His eyes
romantic as aluminium strewn against a sea-wall.
Everyone had to get back. I did,
feeling like a euphemism, and inexplicable.
Everyone explains too much, as the collision of your 'soul'
is gradually moved away. The mad boys laugh
backwards like clouds. Her voice arrests you.
I only want it for the crossword, she says.

The convalescent door raps weakly.
They're selling graceless things,
as the gelati van tinkles past, its lurid music
swerves perspective over. Nothing I need.
The sky pulls into view like a monument.
You declare yourself invalid, but just.
As god comes up on the radar.

Enough to make a woman feel...

Your great gaping knowledge propped on the table,
austere and ludicrous, as someone smoothes the holes
into perfect circles. You eat the Lebanese bread,
hubcap-size in Melbourne, but smaller here.
In the park, the man's arms giddy as a swing
asking asking. You kick your feet into the sky.
I wish he'd just drop dead.

So you sulk out, running your hand along the fence.
Where is the room I woke up in?
The TAB is gleaming like a kitchen.
A dollar each way, you're an heiress now
but shrewd. This is how you do it.
Now aren't the men helpful.

You watch the brick wall coming closer
or is it parliament on air? What's he
looking so indignant about, and since when?
His green skill stopping at the lights,
that business lunch slowing the wheel square
as a weekend. You go home
and do 20 push-ups, as your android sentiments
leaf through the room. Evidence is the last thing you need.

All Our Gods

1

In a quaint abandoned room
night falls, jittery as transmission.
Your exhaustion, cool and stoned, will keep you up
in the hotel, in the ex-students' party.
He's stinking of availability, but it goes,
his dishy way of being dumb but guess-what.
And you're ready. I will love you like Socrates.

The junkies with their sublime shattered faces
are distant and contained. The couples embrace like missionaries.
His soft impartial face tempts you and denies.
Which one? Immoral as the half-hearted
he works at it. Cards languish on his purple table.
Your wonderful calm sets like a limb.
Look at their rattling hearts, and his red mouth.
It's him again, even tomorrow, looking brand-new and startled.

In the drug's shallow pools you go
solid gold like the indoor sun,
aimless and pensive in a plastic chair,
watching the gentle doors.
Your box of moral bones is heavy
and too scrupulous,
ringing out through the naive wood.
He's tender for it.
All our gods are mad and influential.

2

Go on, with your little bits of love,
love him in your hopeless way,
eating the magic party food
you can't imagine being concocted, just existing.
Your mouth, where everything goes in.
He gives you water. Swallow baby.

Solemn and astonished like the Opposition,
you rap against him, cunt-teaser,
wasting all my fucking time. Look at the fragile boys,
they kiss you like a stain.
He's busy. That's six hours down.
You want cocaine like a millionaire.
He gives you fancy food you can stare at for hours.

Wake up in your volcano-sheets, listening
to the murderers cringe. Hold the knife,
what it could go through, as your head conks out
like dead brakes. All your little bits of heart
hold their breath. He throws rocks
in the street, concerned as an insurance company.

The Tenant

The old bloke down the corridor was found today
in his neat and powerless room
with the empty jar of pills.
He was always helpful, except when he was drunk.
I couldn't stand it then,
his ancient sex flapping at his legs
as he fumbled with the door like an idiot
in the afternoon. I suppose it's the suburb
or the age. I never knew what to say to him
much. His daughters never came.
He was his own man, read books,
and had unconventional opinions.
Passing the Sao biscuits over the table
he'd dip them in the tea, and smoke.
The window looked back at the tiny room
like a Health Inspector.
You couldn't explain to the Government.

By Water

Wrap yourself in the tight dead cocoon of your skin.
Did you think it had gone? His face
and the slither of smile all over the room's edge.
His face beneath a pane of water.

Everyone's nice. But who wants to get married?
The music jerks up. Outside you can look at the water.
Here comes that man just dying to tell you his aspirations.
I want to throw up. Where do they make those people?
The men are in love with dead women. I will
blow the soil from your green face, he says. Prop her up.
Who's going to notice? The men cry in a glossy cemetery.

My fleet of dreams will see me home
from the shy charmers, from his bright death.
Half my memory is dream. I remember his third face
washing across night. You are water.
You are the shivering museum glass.

If I Had a Gun

I'd shoot the man who pulled up slowly in his hot car this morning
I'd shoot the man who whistled from his balcony
I'd shoot the man with things dangling over his creepy chest
in the park when I was contemplating the universe
I'd shoot the man who can't look me in the eye
who stares at my boobs when we're talking
who rips me off in the milk-bar and smiles his wet purple smile
who comments on my clothes. I'm not a fucking painting
that needs to be told what it looks like.
who tells me where to put my hands, who wrenches me into position
like a meccano-set, who drags you round like a war
I'd shoot the man who couldn't live without me
I'd shoot the man who thinks it's his turn to be pretty
flashing his skin passively like something I've got
to step into, the man who says *John's a chemistry PhD*
and an ace cricketer, Jane's got rotten legs
who thinks I'm wearing perfume for him
who says *Baby you can really drive* like it's so complicated,
male, his fucking highway, who says *ah but you're like that*
and pats you on the head, who kisses you at the party because
everybody does it, who shoves it up like a nail
I'd shoot the man who can't look after himself
who comes to me for wisdom
who's witty with his mates about heavy things
that wouldn't interest you, who keeps a little time
to be human and tells me, female, his ridiculous
private thoughts. Who sits up in his moderate bed
and says *Was that good* like a menu
who hangs onto you sloppy and thick as a carpet
I'd shoot the man last night who said *Smile honey*
don't look so glum with money swearing from his jacket
and a 3-course meal he prods lazily
who tells me his problems: his girlfriend, his mother,
his wife, his daughter, his sister, his lover
because women will listen to that sort of rubbish
Women are full of compassion and have soft soggy hearts

you can throw up in and no one'll notice
and they won't complain. I'd shoot the man
who thinks he can look like an excavation-site
but you can't, who thinks what you look like's for him
to appraise, to sit back, to talk his intelligent way.
I've got eyes in my fucking head. Who thinks if he's smart
he'll get it in. I'd shoot the man who said
Andrew's dedicated and works hard, Julia's ruthlessly ambitious
who says *I'll introduce you to the ones who know*
with their inert alcoholic eyes
that'll get by, sad, savage, and civilised
who say *you can* like there's a law against it
I'd shoot the man who goes stupid
in his puny abstract how-could-I-refuse-she-needed-me
taking her tatty head in his neutral arms like a pope
I'd shoot the man who pulled up at the lights
who rolled his face articulate as an asylum
and revved the engine, who says *you're paranoid*
with his educated born-to-it calm
who's standing there wasted as a rifle
and explains the world to me. I'd shoot the man who says
Relax honey come and kiss my valium-mouth blue.

Manners of an Astronaut

(1984)

Eliminations

Neither ignorant nor wise
you approach life like Mastermind,
lose, like a soldier, you can;
that hurt note shines through even
this cake of air, accurate, heady.
Each day in your suede jacket
think of this,
your face just swimming,
the damp plank, orbit.

———

Them, being special, cool, and 'liberated',
the lovers, meet,
to talk it over. The kids feel out of place,
this modern adult food won't go down well.

His good qualities can be seen from the island.
It's all lost time. Marry the wind, the table,
a way to be civil, as sun recedes like a tail-light
somewhere, you cumulative bastard.

———

You wake up after the cold shower,
glad that he's gone, your man of the month
has just worn off. Now that's honest.
I didn't like the film, as you argue with the cops
and I lie.

Thick on the ground, the half-baked lunatics
manipulate a word. You've run out of listening
and want to kill, but instead a dream
hangs off like a limb.
Your mouth dislocates his face. I wish you were older.

I can't see anything in this go-slow drug.
Just lucky, I guess, holding his loose helmet,
looking at the architecture.

———

Is that brief pain communication?
My silly soul drives badly round the concourse,
back home, proving everybody wrong, why don't you
crawl out of that damned statue? I didn't mean it,
but there you are, all new and different.
Their stiff rhubarb rubs you up the wrong way, and feels good
like an electric blanket.
The motel purrs like a husband going out.

So What

Separate things are coming at you.
From the front room, cute jazz. Is it?
This slop hovering in the background like a new Hawaii,
and here, for instance, you're communicating things,
but in my head a last hour finds sense
and it becomes what I say it is.
Like his sadness makes you sad. Dumb to feel,
to wonder. If the night wasn't black, would you
with your turning heart, ever listen? Are you?
My dear invention, you can go now.
I've got this much, and your stunned key works.
His brain's small seeds pass for bright.
And downstairs still, music circulates.
I wish the night outside would come in.
Unload the door.
The sufferer may be crowned
but can you sleep like that, your eyes
jutting from door to stair to window,
waiting for that wrist of light to jam or just come home.

Sum

Do I have to look at those sad eyes and feel them
pricking up and drilling, even from there? This muck
that gets between us. Though I wouldn't want to be you
if I thought about it. And it's not muck, anyway,
just inconvenient now to have to think, choose.
In another world, this gesture could be sweet
and you could just stand there, symbolic of things.
But meanwhile, people add things up
and the total is your head. My actions escape me.
I remember water shining like a cage, and not you so much.

The Buddha Speaks

I have reached Nirvana. I have no desires.
I don't want to see you dead anymore, or alive.
This broad uninhabited plateau is heavenly, really.
I have eliminated the possibility of pain.
The slopes are crawling with pain.
Any movement, after all, is futile,
so I have cut down on aid generally
and talked myself out of violent feelings,
like a dense disciple not listening, or worse,
sweeping up everything you say and carefully
sweeping it into his mouth's dump, the words that is.
Those who ask are fools to begin with
so I let my wisdom come out, illustrating it
with little pictures, and my sayings touch those only
who are truly alert. The fools go away no wiser
with their lists and prayers. And my body sits quietly,
emptied of passions.

Lines Written During a Period of Insanity

I

Regret in tears beside you bleeping every 5 minutes.
His mouth, in a permanent sense, seemed logical
when faith broke, but who can forget holes
and these sorrows pouring, or his extra eyes
not touching saintliness but coma. Your experiment works.
No blade is taken like a fridge
to your heart, but walls go away
or get sick. He wraps insight all round the year
then talks. So how can glass be loaded?
That diagram of friends includes a hospital, your head's hopeless
to be with, it feels angled and wrong.

You can sit up forever waiting to resemble 'true'.

II

This wedding's a dream, he will promise jewels, flesh,
but his heart like an angel cries on your yellow door
His eyes are about to go Russian, and love loyalty
and love her given heart, but your house diminishing
out of possible, and why are your yellow hands so naive
and the door meaningless?
Inside, music writhing out of place, why doesn't he scream
green letters out, like that poor seed once, broken, sent, your
            yellow soul
and her white dress, murder,
his lies singing himself out,
but his promise is vacant,
but then death

III

The gorgeous white piano is skidding through the room,
red jazz, and you, pink clarinet no one asked,
not song, but a whole life, and before the stage,
a meal breaks, and some accessible hooligan
mislays this beauty

and now an inkling, suede notes lead in
to this sad set of keys,
and then his break like cars, green clarinet,
collide with me. Go East.
This club is made of flames. But I have watched the walls
lie down like a horizon, raft – your white hands
becoming sea, revolving clarinet, satellite and blue.
Piano beneath the veils.

IV

Remember Europe? Its dust also will lay you.
That record fumbles through scenery. At night on the plain
you walk through stars. And when you've left, your wine
upsets me. You have carried me away. I don't know you.
I don't know why you were making the floor dance.
Don't worry about the door. Don't bother me.
Remember where that faith went? Frail floating paper,
and the kiss you had, dawn was driving into my dreams
with your blue head. Caravan of death, I should let go.
There goes your soul, colt all over the mountains.
Green star, you're mine now.
And fizzing into my mouth, nervous circles sink
these bones of time. Like your face talks from lessons
and you didn't mean it.

V

Sweet hands, don't leave me
in this blindness. You get used to kissing
and liking everything. Regression isn't healthy.
This book has changed my life. Your house,
tortured like an albatross, calls to me
and the bad dream hammers birth and day
apart. I can't tell things, like the tree for instance,
its lock, its green vision riding from air.
White clouds in your room won't go.
The unbearable window keeps nothing, the sky's ghost
coincides with sadness. Only yesterday
I loved you. Today doesn't belong, and you've pressed back.
I'm soaring. Craft of forgetfulness.

VI

You make me travel like Egypt,
but I want to go home. Vain night, I've lost the river.
Your ark sinks, and it's through stars and cords of light,
no mystery, no horizon. The survey was wrong.
You balance on the floor, the cliff is aimless for me,
as tomorrow ticks upstairs. And for my sore eyes, you,
massive claustrophobia, manners of an astronaut.
It would be ridiculous to be happy.
I can't remember where I live.
And why 'rocks'? The sea's wrecked on them.

VII

That dripping note I left for you and the caving yellow house
I still stay in, though it's not there.
This man has spent hours on trains designed to hurt
and now, classic stoned, he chips the conversation up.
Without you, everything has the same silent texture.
Conversation doesn't grab me, and the door's plan of eyes
is throwing you away. There *is* no one else.
The main street may as well be Holland,
the letters ageing in the box

VIII

The uncertain scary rock won't go away.
You think if you go out and practise talking,
it won't be there. But the bed is weighted with it
and the room makes verbs, and the face you drew in me,
not heavy, but constant, sings nonsense,
and these words disjoint. As if I couldn't follow
and this case of brains hits things
and goes out of place.

IX

while you, brave astronaut, don't talk to me.
Her monologue by now is desperate, and points faithfully
into the sky's pit, wandering with children,
and her pink eyes dream,
and her, melting into your dumb ears,
your stupid jacket lying on the couch till it drops.

Manners of an Astronaut

1

Come out from the shower, singing and glorious.
Red light vanishing in the mauve trees.
Gladly enough, your head was only swimming, not president.
The lake with wrath is heavy
and reflections also have made it stop like a screen.
The lake through the white door isn't normal.

2

Bad heart, these 'feelings' fit easily
and move around inside like people at an airport.
The ones that broke out broke me.
Limp jar, you don't make sense, words rattle
in your heart, hit glue, fail.

3

With every vein you've got
worried, a hard clock taking away ghosts.
I heard the day start, not free at that stage
like when I listen to your hand.

The car and them pause.
Inside it they have harboured plots
that bury me with light. As this burden of electricity
gives a temple to my thoughts. You forget fast,
ex-one

4

Grains of madness fall into your bowl of cherishing.
Your heart, virgin and spent.
Cicadas siren in the backyard, can't scream over it
as he picks your equilibrium.
Even the fridge just about faints,
the light wobbling in your blue career.

5

It's not you chafing at my head,
these curled sheets rustling and how long
do these episodes flash for my life,
the pit of it, red, central.
Ash, you can come out.
I saw dawn.
and from the past like a jet, face it, were you.
Painful is the process of return,
Painful his evacuation.
And how sore can you get when you leave water
weighted in gravity, won't swim.

Let's Get Metaphysical

It's party-time in Darlinghurst, but he's sick of hairstyles
and those oracles of fun you give away like nuts.
Here it's raining in the kitchen, his black eyes glimpse virtue.
We hide friends under the bed
and can't get out of the room, stifling and affectionate.
How can you dance with your sprained ankle?
But you can't step back and separate the object from the process.
This thing is beyond love, beyond the brain's split.
The walls are singing with blue love
and the yellow sky dances with me
on days like this.

Enlightenment can't last, its silent smiling adventure.
I thought there was more to you.
The telephone is hot metaphysically
but his material presence is the limit.
What are you doing for lunch? I'm starting a charity until it stops
or else I'm giving it to you. The city like a map
isn't spontaneous. Listen to the lift's electric bell
as people freely pour out, and your free hour
wriggles to the window and jumps.
I don't like it when his body talks.

Half Hill / Half…

1

Deep down of course, the group is gross.
Him being coy is just stupid
but, yeah, you can afford to be,
prying changing skin.
The bars of the street go to the new next place
where your yearly emotion won't come
and don't hail me like letters. You don't need to.
I mean, you've lined the walls and sucked drugs.
Nothing happens when I want you.
Three hours later, phone drama,
and next week, you're lying,
a bunch of success, green ally, that only gets you down

2

The world holds you in place like hairspray.
I walk home stoned, eating my favourite apple,
hearing birds fall out of trees,
super-conscious of walking.
How can you explain boredom in 10 minutes?
I get up from death. The drug's silent avalanche
and the world helping me forget.
What's wrong? ghost of separation
between thought and action.
If you complain here, you're talked out of history.
Suddenly you mean me. Lack of sleep has airbrushed your face.
Forget it, my brain catches up
and clinks callously inside.
This hill my sledge

The Last Interior

(1986)

Extracts from sections 1 and 3

What you love, you end up hating.
The sax plays not smoothly but wisely,
just an edge of anguished moderation.
His seagull piano
landing on the beach
You go breathless, white
The circling wind, lasso

Why are these places so red?
I give you the hand, serene and altarless

————

Good evening, purple spots of the night.
when you finally re-arrive
kicking up gel. Someone gets financially annoying
You can borrow my cigarette
and go out and become blanked.
Skid, the eternal jet firing at the stove.
You've sung *Baby Love* 10 times in the shower.
Your love, your ceremony
juggling rent in an arc of cards
Your shoes stick in a grille
You announce the cake
coming out of the mattress graveyard
No one wears watches
I turn off my obsession
and get bored. The blue sand of your face
like a gate opening its piano

————

You bleat after me through the street.
I sell the Harbour Bridge just to annoy you.
You ring up to tell me what colour my hair is.
My dreams wheel like a poisonous chandelier.

It's like asking the difference between a toothpick and a golfcourse.
Do you want me to explain, *really?*
But you're carping on last night. I don't remember.
You've got New York wrapped up

———

He drops her like a shot.
Safety, princess, with your tear-drop eyes
slow motion come on. 3 suburbs away
I can hear you whisper culture to him,
loads of bars. How do I get to be quaint
like you? Your vicarious chocolates sleeping on the floor.
He's got soft feathers and gives you them
and plays with caution. Alright. Shadows are crawling
up the buildings. But I run silently
hearing all-night videos stun everybody.
Not me, mate. My head's jumping up and down
to look at you. I did imaginary homework.
Dreams care. Go and do what you want
with your brown clothes

Two Monologues

1

Her eyes circle around legends of friends.
She says 'The warmth she gives me fills me'
collapsing in the chair. She says 'I walked in,
'65, alone, you know, hair to here', looking past him,
'our arms collapsing, one of the (emphasis) few
really good people.' Next to her, the lefty
like a yacht so fucking up himself. His hopeless girlfriend
looking 10 years in the eye, and cautiously, respect
rings her glass. She means feminist, arguing
with his king, making sure her shoes,
going home, his heartless rhetoric. Poignantly.
Drugs, you make the horseshoe bar look worse.
The men look down from their age and scoff.
Sure, the moratorium. Sure, the lawn with placards.
Power drinks itself into 'the next fuck'.
First you find promiscuity liberating,
then after a while you have to liberate yourself from promiscuity,
debilitating object.

2

He's good value, really
remarkably sober because
remarkably broke but he can hold it
He says you know she's one of those people
that've got no sex, just a ball rolling down a hill
getting older and older, just a ball
collecting wrinkles until it's so swarming
and dies. There's rain you can't hear, real light.
You can't buy anything for anyone.
Those stars weren't true. I mean, money?
That was the 10 I got off Cartridge
a head entirely square.
You don't want to pour your favourite beverage into that, do you?
He sticks glasses in the sink.
A mild bloke, that one,
and bundles down the corridor
whistling Milk Cow Blues

63 years

After being amusing for so long, she changes the position
of her legs and brings him back
Her eyes, timid and defiant, filter backwards through the children,
the emptied bed, she ploughed on
My religion's too strong in me, though he turned at the end,
a gesture. He was that sort, you know,
£5, you got roses.
the handsomest man I ever.
And the mother falls from her, and the strong old woman,
as she brims for a bit in the dropped room
We got married 3 months later.
No one could predict it.
took the kids to church, though he wasn't one himself.
Life's, yes, just a great sort of gap.
You wouldn't believe the things.
as she puts away softness.
You could talk about anything.
when her arms were kissed and loaded.
Life's impossible without him.

22 years

There's something I don't know what it is
which I've stopped doing somewhere along the line.
I just don't give off the same stuff.
I mean when you've been through some loungeroom, all his mates
lined up, not the faintest idea where you are, how to get out
So it's just fear that creeps up my neckline
I've been observing other women to see what sort of things
they do, you know, coocheying a certain way,
taking a cigarette and I try but when it comes
to it I want to flee out the window
or Right. Go. Go. That's it, boy.
But you can't do that sort of thing.
I mean, do you act a certain way. What is it?
I mean that's not correct etiquette is it. If I
could just find out the correct behaviour, the pattern,
and learn it and learn it

29 years

'I only like women who're interesting
She sits at my feet, praying and propping
and tells nil basically. May as well be a magazine
except she doesn't get instructed and go out'
He twiddles his degree and then his hat.
How does contemporary mean effort? The log slopes in and out
of the fire. 'But they don't like me. I've lost the boy.
Yeah, I got an index at the back of my head
where they met, cutting my hair. You two go mad,
attending to it.' She tries to change his sex
so she can love it.

25 years Always

The children I cradled in my curled body,
their shiny limbs dropping into sleep.
Dream, repair. I protect you with watching.
These arms support a head
I carry them to bed, one by one

Excavation
(arguments and monologues)

(1990)

On first looking into Fairfax's Herald

Mr Gromyko observes Washington's autumn rain,
2 Sakharov Place, the Russian Embassy.
Subtly re-named, for those who didn't notice.
Mr Shultz, harbinger of peace, comments modestly.
It's all reported like a slide-rule adjusted by the President.
Simultaneously, General Ortega doesn't get much coverage.
US mercenaries?
Mr Shultz piously knights the street.
Simultaneously, the Air Force, fingering its report,
desires what's feasible –
a last blast from a dead country.
The President builds a hideout for his bombs.
We play dead.
They surge up like coffins through our graves.

1965

The river winding red and green with corpses
She told me
They stood them on the banks
and shot them
anyone vaguely suspected of associating with, belonging to,
sympathising with, the PKI
the largest communist party in a non-communist country
in the world
in Indonesia in 1965
The useless President, blinded and blinded,
shot, in anther way
The false counter-plot making the original lie
seem true
Blood and rotting, you could smell it
she told me, crying, rivery
out of earshot
We keep the books, the names, hope
in our heads
The blocked rivers trailing like glaciers
The army's fear like a slowworm
eating away at my parents, my sisters, my brothers
We could've been voted in
The millions of Opposition glues powerlessly together
This President? Tin.
Crying
out of earshot
The thick rivers we parcel in our heads.
Whispering.
in Indonesia in 1965

Excavation Excavation

1

I go out and get more smack
I watch her pull it out of her trousers
her washed-out Cross face hands me the sweet drink
for a second
we rap the blue car
in the blue light, and complain when we feel it
the crumby amount, but shoot home
Anything to make you seem less
When I finally broke out of my bridge
and made an idiot, as you
go away, you look small and ugly
so I hate you, raising your liar voice
your softened-up entourage. I hear.
your petty socialism swamp the backyards

2

At home we hit up a sort of passionate sadness
Joy a write-off that I had once for you
Machiavelli, your face is screwed up
He builds an altar, burning to his friend
When it ruins my blood I feel good
and listening to you, well I don't have to
So what? Some girl was mean to you once.
I prefer the strangers here,
steaming my heart off like a stamp.

3

What you do is Christian, not longing
His cups break
when I think of you
The sun sets at half past eight
I hide to get out of it
It's best to repress rather than
pour it onto the wrong person

I mean, we both want boys
I look in the gutter
but I got stained
My breasts get heavy with desire

4

You're pathetic,
the way you heave your heart
over some buoyed-up deadshit
I watch all the yellow in my glass shake.
What do you expect? really?
His soft girlfriend strokes his furrowed brow
behind some white fence, lawn-mowing.
He cradles his soft child-bride
I jerk at every car

5

He came to an agreement and
you know
I'm relieved really,
having just conjured it all anyway
He knots his head down into his guitar
everything's misaligned
I haven't achieved what by now I should've
he says I don't know your eyes are always blazing
Still, I never slept so well
and today, the travelling trees
remember leaving, the perplexed harbour
I woke up, laced with sorrow, mother

Napoleon

True love's a big pain
I look at you and laugh
at your martial domesticity
Guns answer the phone
but I never learn
Your sloppy relationship waggles off, suburban and banal
When I look at you I get harder

You lower the will into a pile of drugs
If it'd smash him I'd live it
but instead a stuck radius
that drivels towards you
whom I love and swap
your blue face flags,
the neat dawn makes me sick as it coats you
like a net. Property tells me to fuck off
so I lose Austria. Go and kiss her
level. The head blows in its socket.

Penelope

An ordeal,
to separate red from yellow
I see you go down before my eyes
a sweet narcotic mixture
Your eyes don't stop anywhere
He palsies with the crowd
Next door she cries in his paper arms
You think dumbness means honest
and wrap it up with your attempts at humanism,
loving and serious.
or is she laughing? I dream of you
a host, a shaft, a wedge
that next day burdens out
Will and obsession equal science
it binds these Stalin-bones, memories
And you splat out so far you're desolated
Pragmatism culls
Hard lake, glass, I looked it over
I turned it in my eyes like a computer
But, yeah, she talks sense
cooped-up in bed

A soft worm of selflessness nestles and curls inside her,
take it into your soft heart
cursed and forgetful.
My love withdraws like an army
a slow asp of words seethes in the white crack of your elbow

My heart flaps out of its fish-tank
in the middle of conversation
imagining every noise
near you
every trivial honour I come up with

Stoically, I watch your ghost ship blown back
from the bay
The white-armed women hold me in failure
rubbing from my eyes
the heart a rack of ice
and I forget

I'm law if this is waiting
I watch the videos of dead
the wraiths of love I limit
like car-sickness
Being eulogised, they slide into the horizon like a coin
The world gets out of it
and goes to bed.
You could've been shimmering in his arms
with a new code of pragmatism
Stop tears with coke
Limp home to another *baby*.
Proportionately, you're strong
winding him into bed
My brain's pillars cave in under last week
Eyes a river flooding in a blindfold round your head,
a mask, an opening.
Perfect, meanwhile, turns in her arms like a key

Love Sucks

1

Past care
I don't want a bar of him
Your mate gets fresh again
I go back to the mysteries of science
that pass you in splendour
and what I aver naturally
I now consign
We clear the table's fluoro books
to mull drugs
When glass wears off, it stinks
I leave your desert in a shot

2

He finally remembers
the brat behind her hair is inconsiderate
clagging up the room
Her traffic sponges as the lines turf out
He rolls over
She motor-mouths until the birds crack
A charade for breakfast / then you go to work
(We stared for about a year)
She hits him with opinions like a clam
Love sucks

Six Goodbyes

1

His cursory So long
To me, shame, dishonour
frazzle down the drain
as truth is eloquent, passive and detached
I plug his mouth with venom
the phone's rash
Desire and remorse confess together
past caring
I wade through the grey trees
cradling death

2

New streets tinder to the harbour
They clean up simultaneously in the maverick flats
Two streets away, cars droll towards the Cross
Saturday's a trial
Emptiness follows all the yachts
The capitalists are friendly when you buy
'Shakespeare saw that it…was the perfection of a woman
to be characterless' (Coleridge reflects)
My ears are stuffed with men and the noise they make
A girl walks down the used lane with her pay

3

The foamy ingenuous girls kiss and flirt
True love grapples with it forceps and ekes out
what sense you had
They clamour for attention
and in the gin dark I think only of you
as Consolation heckles
Downstairs, the taps chore, and he bashes off to work
His kisses don't work

4

She laughs with the cherub women
She loses faith and goes
after melting the drugs and administering
I stick the union that we had once in my head
but carry home the sorrow root, the sac

5

Surf music seeps from the separated father's flat
A madman in the lane shouts nothing
The walls shudder with the traffic
The Government doesn't know you from a bar
I plug my ears with wax to hear the sirens
Every second weekend his kids invent a yard
between stumps of furniture, a tin shed and a gate
The fridge is tanked with frost

6

This junk does nothing
The rotating lounge room and the American music fan out
The flat's coffin works your heart's tin bureau
What I eat I throw out like a philanthropist
blasé with the routine
The dangling acquiescent dawn crops up

Elegy (I)

The safe idealists love the impossible
its regal garb shields from the ash
of television. At first, I was open like a wound
and let knowledge find its Lethe's
washed your blood. I wake up from a slag of love
The trees crimp in the sky

Her lizard hands weld him with its trowel and tin
and slopes into the catered bed
It's a good time
when you're told off by the guard
A million brained commandments war and wince
I prefer the squally music to your frozen world
I give back the trough he feeds me
She oracles and knits
It wasn't, in the end, much chop
They possy up some thick recruit, or a party
Life's good without you

Disinformation

1

The fireworks of peace and celebration go up in the harbour
above the warships. Sailors strut through town
adored by skint women who, for a job, will cheer their garish flag
One's trippy and bursts into the flat
jawing the air with a knife
He was disinformed. The pictures, the hype
that rev a plane across the Gulf of Sidra
mill in his baseball head until Intelligence chucks him

2

Our clown Prime Minister jostles on the steps,
unable to dissemble,
unable to not be loved by Indonesia, France, Chile, China
He troths the Bases, not alienated anymore
He clucks his timely personality
The sin of doubt assails the booths
He holds his broken minister in a camera grip
and weeps a tub
'Your women are beautiful', says the Yank
in relay with his Navy darkening the harbour

Achilleus

Dawn breaks through the droog blanket's chipped flavour
as another slam beams its cuts on his face
The knife clicks in its cask The purple teetering globe
'He kicked me good Now I won't bash for a while'
He rolls and spills repeating love's dumb elixir
I fall in his stoked house
on love's conventions
your heavy heart obsolescent metal
budget and proclaim

Perpetually a drag
Music greases its haggard souvenir
The muffled snow flicks down
and reckons you're clapped in death
I watch the fight from the brown shore
The two in my head turn like a supermarket

I don't know what close means, being dead all a life
Whatever comes, comes. Unergonomically, you crawl
in bed the sad cathedrals He looks at the gun windows
Writing swims into its pin
my mother's white sea-shells
the slicing river

Newtown Pastoral

1

He tells me about his pet turtle
and the pregnant daughter next door
She sits on the verandah in the street
smoking in the sun
I've been scabbing off my girl
so I give her rocks
The last one sent me spiralled
They caved in on the beach knocking their guns
My old man says you must make a concerted effort
The take-home pay's shit

2

You can hear him pottering around at 4 o'clock
his pet animal reacting to the phone, the wind
At dawn kids skate past
Her head comes up through the ice in her coat
Dingy customers plonk themselves on the doorstep
and scrape
Either way it's a joke
A basin of pity kills me to the top
Amongst the lovers and the nylon flowers

Kings Cross Pastoral

When she remembers every chumpy thing
the baby weather hurts her, the sick sun
At home a dead blind flaps from its joint
She goes on,
like it's the latest reason or excuse
and hibernates with pity's taxied screen around her
I could cop it if it worked
She jilts the door, roneo'd with debts
Thought protects you from the street's chattels
The sky passes like a stick

A regular tip his crinkled rites of love
Joy cacks itself laughing
and with these crimes I shut the door
having gone off pity
The heart's anchor's dust now when he shows up
harmless, dishonest, recent
A car is better than a tree
Voices fall on the city's spine and crack

Panegyric

'At first it was one big gala, but now it's worn.
We kiss through a covenant of tears
I've tried to slake it. You charge and drop
from hyper to a pool. I reckon we should kill it,' he says,
crunching up and crying.
The moon rises in its dish.
'You didn't lie, but all the same it's foiled
I fell into the sum
and now your era, your ride, closes to the max.'

Pure and Applied

(1998)

'Of course it was their armour dragged them down'
The Battle of Trasimene, Martin Johnston (1947-90)

'Is prevention better than cure? Is Canberra?'
The Joyful Mysteries, John Forbes (1950-98)

Pure and Applied

1

The channel caves in his hand like a weak cushion
as news reads the screen
and curved along its poverty, a reflecting and equivalent desert
occupies geometry
which devalues each tincture my chatelaine
which people vacancy
like today's harping and the litmus of his hair

2

Politicians nod like priests
You slip in the crowded chair like 3 million others
TV shows you
The rest is dreck, a slump
You surrender to his embalming pill
his glorious forgotten blockout kiss and nest
The walls' diagrams arrowing to a former heaven peter in the mind
Monotonous branches scratch the ditchy air
I had to look at 800 dollars
but death precedes me entering like worthlessness

3 (the good weekend)

Ten pages on a headache A world satisfied by charisma
The corner shop's dim globes the newspaper's parting atoms
but death can be 'egotistical, manipulative', his claim and corona
Her burying mother acridly grinds into the present
An article probes the shops, the ultras
in the sad dark regions and recesses of his relation

The sheets wind milky green
and then a big blue sky's supposed to incize
putting you in the right counsel
I watch his weakness strive and shut

as theory wades, but on practice it's a klutz
I protect him from ardour
Here, in this propensity, this rust
My paraphernalia crash in a junction of boredom

   4

Automatically he'd be a lump
The light's suicide split craving beneath the wax door
Piano tinkles over the woolknit-lounge ad, his thoughts
that mirror a wreath of gloss abrupt pages
perspex and disheartened and foam
dead desire
and he uncrumples from the black lacquer

   5 (sum)

'It bores me severely
Everything you say is thrashed into a refrained verdict
numbfully secure at its post
The car's underwater the doorkey starts
and recedes like a gun, excellently
and never loved. Obstruct, by all means, any silent rack or behest
Anyway, it was major which you blasted, a real user

He was glamourised, delta'd, totally miami'd
like a shoot-out, you know, head above water
His blue hair shining like rockets
Dance-a-rama *I'll* say, you should've seen the gronks
they turned away in squadrons, rapturously
to the new spasmic floor. I could've killed
but I dropped stuff instead
and was, subsequently, messed for any social, being severely zomboid
Last night: what a crack'

Autumn

You go to bed a failure and rise a saint
The casino's trays of lights wobble in the river
Unpack the origami news in prison flats
and books advertised like cars
TV tracks the angst-ridden comedian's path
I forget who I am, and drive
or hover at a desk, a blank mosaic
while their shocks comfort and defer
She retires to her studio
with her devices and rueful catharsis
Dust words blow away
The time you waste
murky and naive, the plinking church organ
and sweet liturgy pouring on the air
A beautiful object covers his book
Concrete rain falls down

And let this conglomeration go

My brother's pulling voice falls around my maps and factories
I drift
His tournaments of innocence preserved forever
Each has put a ring around the heart I bang
to constrict, to satisfy. They train the blood away
I clog up into armoured space, all notions

and don't feel better after sleep coming back
with its new twist of incongruity, the statue park he
clouds me, painful longing arms
I watch the photos table and dissolve
his electric accordion whines through the Metro
and each white layer adores, puerile and futile

the artificial tourists like me queue up
while in Sydney you're entirely stoned, an odalisque, an impediment
to all my traps, adventures, spans, bereavements, conglomerations
Green horses kick the snowing walls
Another draughty foray, a blight of regret
veers between fluency and sorrow
amongst the pulchritudinous
in the carved green high wet land
I walk through the museums more dead

London Saver

My cortex dissolves its crisp moon imploring like a painting
and went out on the wrong drug
New Year's Eve they just sat there We were cracking
the worst we got was a stony peck
At home you'd be floorboarded The boss's a real tumbler
showers like birthdays
Still we had the hash He thinks it's garlic
The others were a bit sarc-y but you end up friends
in these war rooms I look out at the greyness and save more
probably Istanbul or Spain the guys're divine
There used to be an eleven but they've all pitched off
into Outer Mongolia or something She throws the fags
It was lashing everywhere when I clicked the tickets
deciding on a country Her dust voice He was a jerk a retread
If you want a shower I'll sneak you through
Another cover pours from the system
Give the club scene a miss Acid's died in the arse
I don't really go in for all that non-discrimination sensuous shit
Still we were total'd in Summer
I put away about 50 a week double-shifts married to the pub
She shivered I listen to their diminishing brain cells
and the sloppy histrionic hotel music like a church

Voyage

Two Winters

I learn at the museum Van Gogh is never cold
The young painters talk a lot
At home he's stoned in glory
The grand lines of the shopping arcades warm and lose me
He deals out the photos like cards
I walk beneath the wriggling towering statues
the silky skating water's shattered pews of orange light
letters dating and rusting
His lying singing voice warbles but nothing hurts me
Advertising welcomes the cold travellers

I remember his black sweat hair and lava
and hammering in his head like mud
The buildings slant in the canals
silk mirrors craven and broke
Without him I feel empty and alive
the happy eighteenth-century clocks, the desk skulls

Still Life

Spongy beer shells the brain's late noon
Close the window on the tortured cats' feudal sex
The cash register below rings like a phone
The weather inside's cold though outside's blue
away from other peoples' blur
Pop songs in imitation English prate and hustle
The flowers are new like plastic

Guitar's secluded jazz pierces the rain,
the white mist, as cities disappear, plate islands
cracking in the sink It takes me down its ladders
all my fallow desires his green-blue skin's
anguish and trial. And here the earth's soot

returns that drawer of worms
that mattock I kicked, bled
into the fourth death into your rig
these ranks of love that tweak and ruction
each collapsing prince and rocks

and console myself with murder's green chiffon hands
and shovel highly if grace's jot anoints
my head's dope and quandary jig the sticking water in its cup
remembering all our clanking trestles, instruments, switches, vaults, taps
and clag the blue Antarctic cremating all he digs
to skin these ghosts
Instead I had him like a brooch and charity and lies

Voyage

1

Bitterness and rancour lathe inside
the heart's bowled walls
Persuasion thwarts
Money doles its hindrance
In a purdah of sorrow and revenge
I listen to the wailing mosques

2

and spread out on the galling Irish Sea's grey tide
a sinker a match
The boat rocks me in its traitors and feathers
She turns to amber in his arms
His beauty turns its ringing empty vessel

3

I looked for beauty's porch and cave
along the brainy coasts the sparkling cities' griefs
that suck my holes or heart
The simmering road gets lost and all these boxes
The future was a mess Come back in crates and dreams
The stone cross on the whining hill was fire
I stand in your red paddocks like a scarecrow
sliding through the graves
Each ocean was the one I left
and I was blown like rice

Forfeit

1

Unreal world I see from the cave with opinion, change and decay
and then the blinding forms
I wake up in a sty
in all the wet satin rivers
The shifting stars that move you further
I keel on, scraping out the fog
'Affliction is the way'
your voice a stone that summits and sinks
your green mouth is in my skin
I have to yield
my painstaking and ridges

2

Europe's jewels cowl in another smothered sunset
Health's pavid I echo with his minions
You blurt out vocatives and credentials
That house's mire That drubbed life
Your flash weakness a tribute to his cause
These pegs these languages travail

and toll constantly on him, a procession of him
in jeopardy in the tipped canals
his suspended film unrolls, sleep's prison
I look west to the horizon's walls of brass
and seem to see my sod and quick life frittered
in denizens of quasi-love, curriculum,
and rail against the stones, the bright-blue oscillating sea
and breathe hope's cud whereby my gain, lover's lack
that doped me, sweat and plaques
that lounged my shady stew
that splits my life's purchase like a sack
and go with the 'appointed to tribulation'
The creaking parched water saddles and repents
He moans across the oceans and his voice was like a pilaster

Impresario

1

Spiritualism's amnesia quells your desires and regrets
My commerce is with the dead
The safe classics draw out their golden gates
For sociological reasons you view the overseas artists
Ascetically you throw away the status symbols
the car the boyfriend
and medicine the place

At work screens drill into my eyes
Saints float across the ceiling up to heaven
not like now's mutual exploitation
The water's magnetic tape stripes to the horizon
blinding and unhindered

2

and environment the floor in his communal domestic
where theory binges its archetype of doom
and rodeo my heart around his molten shore
Desire scams They're stressed I'm bored

The feather of justice rings up on the scale
and his dearth's slapped across the miner's pan
and still calls from the street the meter and the clock are equal
Unexotic, I buy you cans

Work spills into arithmetic
and cries for virtue's blue writ
the cold pizza breakfast by the bed
The soft clasp of his mouth that dredged me spared me

3

He turns back to the quiet bowling green
the ape electrics
and fits like safety, touched, amenable, locked-up
He looks at the guitar like a chiropractor
The sour lost wind slips off into a kinder grip

Capitalism's pity leases out our rights
The conductor's solitude, the newsreaders' rapport
News carves the unions up
His hair's different now
She cares like I used to want to
Their donor understanding perishes you
immortal like plastic
I floor it in a ditch
The cockroach crawls inside the clock
Now he 'supports' me when he used to love me
The actors act across the screen
There's nothing I have to cut off or distract me

4

He fills the music every black motive
he ascribes
wade in the dead water a playboy a cautionary tale
I drive through the swift memories
his broad variety
now life runs its useless gamut's timber

mysterious like an idiot
The talking people bask in the kitchen
their highlight a scratch
drugged and regressive
Amongst the flowers and burnished air
when love and him were new

New Corral (August 1992)

America readies for its new corral
while elsewhere patriots kill their way to truth
One sticky flag guns down another
The flagpole sticks with blood
Between golf and fishing he sees the recent poll
and how when guns and deaths were flashing like an ad
respect went up and TV made a mint
Fearing, he swaggers. The crowd's muzzle and pebble fade
His cabled mind, reeling a polluted catch,
opts to clear the barn
and send the Christmas kids to plough the wounded down
to smooth the twitchy rag white ditch with tanks
(The odd untidy charred arm can be cut)
He charts across the course now
furrowing an aluminium club, and swings
and squints into vacation sun
Vietnam could recede, he tees, and failure
and Boy the country thought as one then
tipped and vacuumed on TV's dish
His pretzel heart wheels into resolve on the ninth hole
and springs from the buggy for the news

Last Class

Fear that I may not impart what's crucial
halts the class. In fairness to old Professor Talbot
(whom I never liked and who reciprocated)
I look up at my cold windows
and forty years have stumped the quote
Have I done well?
The students poke their sheets
There was a book to write
but somehow years were shaded
Time whistles at the University's gates
the spinning gargoyles and the stretching stone gods point and warned
Brown and yellow leaves fall down
By 5 it's dark and rain. Am I the one I was
reeling at the other end of time
who thought his teachers gods?
Has all I've learnt transferred?
Is knowledge now a chore?

On flight

Every shore I land is ice
Every dream's his skin
Where horses pound, gold rolls
to rip my purpose out

I turn against the sun and ply
the round world's cape and brim
but where I traipse, lies follow

His apotheosis now revoked
Gods crash undone
Squared brick shows where marble was
Come down the hill's soft side
Here the ancient senate house
I fought for task and deed

Rostra

At dawn sirens start
Zips of day shrivel through blinds
over the next wall and the bed
White haze across the hills of flats
Aerials wobble through heat
Downstairs they fight, next door they love
The lift-well trims and cranks
through each floor's advocates
The porter smokes in his frieze
Boats of rubbish trawl up the street's prow
Shops unfurl, assistants guard their gods
Vines hang from the lane's arch
Market prices sing
as veils of goods dull you
smarting on the year's first blast
gifts that staunch
cheer that lays

your strife
Death's bones inside the door

———

Dreams and systems lapse
Jars fill with pettiness and schemes
Error and confusion halt

a chilled brocade
Rows break through the floor
their advocate of dust

———

The city's rising roof-line cemetery of metal crosses
Each block a Calvary to every prospect
Radio claws obstructions through the walls in clattered sentiment
Announcers stint each verge, each bode
you fix or bother
Grim pitcher slopped with flats, cheers, stops

———

We came in bright awakening
Forgery and fate were crinkled panes of sea
The dead enrich the soil with their ruin

Forum

Next door they sigh and bind
Life's train and crypt and pressing hands are shunting to the square
Bells chink over traffic
With no wounds to wipe, you tick off the contented spread of dead

Sun moves North along the balcony each day
Ghosts walk the falling streets
and reach the 16th Century's reliquaries and clash
that flare the metal globe
the high snow the white green mountains
Alcoves shelter raw water's salt and weeds

This cheer that hides despair
as all that's burnt and meagre gaily trills
Slide off, rich day, cares and hours wait
back to the cortège flats'
silo of memories, night's pharmaceutical brilliance
chips bones along the floor's marbled array
Walls of melting empires
grading into darkness
on water's gold and green crossing swords

Venerdi Santo

Green birds play on terrace weeds
Shadows swipe the flat
Keen on profit, shops stay open through the hours of agony
Pigeons clack and echo in the eaves
The shrieking water heater punches
Cabinets of desires chase each painting's plight and gorge

I search through the black ditch while she talks
The street sinks. Sun shines on lightness
The old chill returns like a friend
Go down through crypts and slabs
Centuries fall away
Above, small voices ring, coins fade

Day falls calmly down behind the thorn-crowned flats
Spools of flowers my ring my sheet
The dreams' confiding friends guide me to the source
Loves fall like wax
A gold hooded skeleton flails in marble sheets
holding the only key in mocking bones
in night's cracks

Travellers from the New World

The folks expect you to kiss the sod in Ireland
I tried to feel their link and pith
England was antipodean must
Switzerland was grouse We stayed with friends
Our Italian's micron I guess we lose a lot
but you've got to check the plate
They should just cordon off the Northern hemisphere
and charge admission in
I used to wonder how they re-created stuff
An American to the husband 'You do the outside I'll go in'
filming the believers Churches sack me
It doesn't seem right sonking through to art
Same for that Egyptian plea, the sleeping dead
Furs weigh past each shop of gold
You shell out beggars and chill It's intense
the accessory food a mask
I thought there'd be more history here

Traffic

London's rain steams
Tourists roll their crying cameras
in the hotel's shot collection of trips and drowned
Your last money catches on the news
Continents away the same stars hooked and fell
Languages float behind each desk
Foreign tears, love a trick
above your chains of things
The river stretches out to jump
Lament in every gnashing seat
knowing when I plight or talk
the plot we'd cede
Languages shuffle
bingeing through traffic
which turns on terror and freezes
over the tipped atlas's
brigade of memories drab and polished like television
then only cars rustling and birds pinching night
having sat for days in a vinyl room Countries wither
Snow and sunrise in another hemisphere
my pilgrimage my dictionary

Ruin Among the Lovers

Does it matter when she ignores your ardour
clinging as it does to every dead minute
sucked into the sliding fax rolls
and the tinted office
You return to shrunken houses where love packed

We play bridge in the food suburbs
They practise their performance on a shelf
Screams and dribbling water conceptually groove
Minimalists criticise the lights
Foreseeing ruin you ruin everything

Estate Agents smile over the frilly houses
their arms hosting the new doors
each listed fitting ticked and spoken
Rent climbs the picnic rooms
You tie the car together and drive to another valley
blunt windows the phone's dead line sawing endless messages
each street familiarized and invisible
She reprieves crumpled action
which walks from love in ashes
Silent rain crosses over years
He strikes out of the world

Interest Rates

1

'I used to be like you, full of icy self-regard
but life monotonously catches up and culls you
and all the others' Things begin to glow
like your own house, car, and love's equivalent
You get sick of being alone and raddled, and he's a real pet
...isn't he? So I buckled under, got a richly job
and I'm, you know, fulfilled. Before it was just a covey of
        unrealistic aims
Everybody told me.
He dusted me off
who had once been lost
Now it's solid, tangible
The baby's like cement to me
Otherwise the million things I wanted every cider brick
I'd just be drifting or immersed'

2

'You can score easily in Thailand
but the stuff's no def for me'
Her drugged voice matinees and peels
She parks the dryer and puts the sixth gin down
after two pre-spiritualism weeks
'There I can withdraw from this chemical western mew
Drugs and alcohol and sex rivet you in place
but in the East they starve and grow, I mean spiritually
They have truth and peace and death and acceptance'
The god advertisements sheep in between the sitcoms
and the Government making strikes illegal
She looks at the cleaner stove
'Europe was a blast but this's cheaper'

3

The artist observes her attitude
and her observation equals the product
which we can't get Personality's enough
Her head knocks in its shell
'I mean, you're not a bimbo' he says, profoundly
'and for the last two hours on Ecstasy I thought yeah
right She's/It's got to be' she listens through the beer stool
through his petulance to Adeva's geometry and slings
His bones and crystals jump and prig the laser stairs
He would be at it with its ghosts of peace
and Truth roaming empty and haranguing
her supple rhododendron mantra's steel jailed corridors
The console shards 'I mean, I was majorly transformed'
insight levies Each pringle of expense continues
its buffet-car of depth's serene atlas joy
The greasy boards and lights and mortgage
dull the disc.

Eating Vietnamese

'I've got a lot of doubts but he's so considerate
I'm looking for a psych
to work through. He's digital
where I'm a klutz, but living out of bags
was just too gross, scatting home to change
and then work
I'm trying to get him to smooth the place
You should stay too. The country's lush
I want to hammer on my own for once
This restaurant's divine They're refugees
Asians are beautiful don't you think, quite hairless
She wore apricot chiffon There were kids everywhere
So demanding. Am I missing?
I guess you're going to soon
These places make me horny
It's honest to see the way they kill'

The hands that burned

They cavort in loving grass
Black complaining smoke ruins the landscape
They dance for the good watches he gets at work
his boring tiring camp job
but the town's richer
The kind guard shoots between the eyes
Obligingly, he casts the babies up
At night he listens to her growing stomach
The priest absolves for goods
'We burn them' he answers
between loving kisses. He says 'It was hard for me,
they beat my brother up.
Our choir's good.' Christmas carols rise over the snow
perfectly
'The train tracks – always blood, and messy
for the town
The food's good, the pay easy, conditions lenient'
She loved his shining face when he shot the huddled man
in her pretty town
'if only the smell, the clashing trains
would leave, but trade's robust
and kisses sweet where love swans
past fresh walls, beneath new pines'
beneath the crackling noise
in gentle Treblinka

Achilleus to Odysseus

Vanished day,
to strive for fame, to glitter in a marble pool
but lose the task
You sit among the virtuous weeding out life
Personalities sulk
the talking breakfast, the blacked-out calendar
They whirl and fit

I wish I lived with silence
black waves plucking the shore away from things
Traffic stripes night and trains kick
the black dissolving world
and stove-white pages
Drunken introverts graft home
the active and idle
Velvet bodies forming on the beach
Footsteps break the slab of flats
I walk into a house of death

Petronius Arbiter in 1997

Do you like the jacket? I've just gone spare on clothes
Materialism brooks and tastes after failure's screed
I'm post-delinquence. When money checked
I trashed it like a source, truth's zenith
I slate through the clubs, looking mint
where keen girls spot me like a crier on a plinth
a plastic card to deck, while spacey actors shift
But her cutting edge china, dinner an aubergine –
I undid the knot. I wish I was a saint
The writing comes all day in clots
I'm so drama. The air pinked passion
then devastation on a tab
All night I was conveyed, lobbied
to make a lesser mortal halt –
fabulous bachelor, equerry of doubts
Her tragic suit campaigned
I was a grill of twigs, a nong, jabbering in a convoy
across the nobbled cans of rooms, fortuitously loaded
My friends in languid pairs bucket me
ark couples bearing soapy news and kids
I prefer to be open and arise

after Sappho

He seems to me to be like a god
him, if it's fated, to be above a god
who talks softly with you
bending close and smiling easily

This tears me
at whose sight my tongue dries
and my voice catches

Straight through a thin flame
twines down my limbs
My eyes are fixed
and the air thuds
and breath extinguished

And sweat runs down my limbs, fever
shimmers paler than glass
I feel myself changed and turned
towards death

Night and Day

Trite yearning expels its medals
Mortal sins hold me in their frame which shrinks me
It was nice, then you run in chains
ultimate compromise
You can sit for hours and listen to his clothes
He scoffs at my art. I freeze at home.
In another flat, he sips his dose
and scratches out silence
Wind climbs the traffic stars
the city's trim horror you praise like a servant
noises folding distance
I press my hands to the gas bill

Soft voices impale
He tells of his achievements
and 'confirms' your existence
in his parliament
Funeral birds break
the sky's white mortar
pouring down its tremors. Parks drip,
the sliding cars despair should rake

He extrapolates

1

It's not that I bent to her will,
or changed in any elemental way, but to keep the peace,
to keep her, I postponed opinion, let it hover in my head
and not protrude into our clinch. For her
everything was definite. I tend to be less set –
flowers and knives chatter in me. She couldn't hear
above the din of definition how I was slipping off.
Evidence and application were her fields,
I liked the scrawls they made
Motivation slept, books draped
then I had depressed and it was grey
the ashtray CDs hanged like cards

2

Time ticks through the hot and cold water flats
I love the Rwandan CD I don't espouse
The pygmy tribe they found was great
I concentrate to remember those I'm with
If I could, I would sing of love
Aspiring, unsuccessfully, to wealth
I stay home and hear her saga mope and taiwan blinds ladder sleep

Green Target

When media fizz, silence expands
back to the clamped grass and china leaves
I scramble through my tax
to find I've eaten rent and paid with thought
I mean I'm happy that he's happy
his ornate voices mash and ripple
It went like the jeopardizing stars
His husband attentiveness
amidst the democratic gossip
Unregarded catalogues pile up
Cars squeal and ring
Favoured love falls through dreams
You cry until they go, yank happiness
back to life's clocked cell
vaguely listening to the sliding ocean's soft detergent foam.

Electra to Orestes

(to a friend, leaving)

My friend, before we met I was in pain
as one who loved me I could not requite
and so pretended for some paltry gain
of status, satire, end to cabled night,
to return affection when faith had shone
its last extinguished prick – then this was made –
faithless sand he built an edifice on
and I colluded, mired in false trade.
Then recognition blasted into wit
to apprehend what I had thought had died
for true love souvenirs and now unfit
to love, but now you prove me wrong who ride
the ceaseless world, not injured but inured
to former life. How have I since endured?

Who Praise You

When I see his face it's as if it were always there
and my eyes stop tunnelling past people and rooms
and stop at him like a mirror
But I pass, speechless
Those around him talk closely
My head bows down its pang of glory and torn eyes
when the room empties
Where should I go to hear your voices
to see your skin like bright paper,
me, unable to speak? The streets torment
and people bunch,
windows and hope slip by
More alive than myself
which night closes

Two Leaders

1

The nice President tells us what to do
which torch joined us
Our Prime Minister shuffles and prevaricates
Let's lose the black armband glitch of history
and praise our forebears, clanking through shiny trees
and taming soil. Here we plant democracy
Our white fathers sit voting and amending in the chambers
Our mandate's been enforced
after minorities and charity
Now fearless statements rub

2

Beneath the market dome he inspects his empire
Patrons coil on the rich statues
He throws sand
while hospitals stagger and schools cut
at each decree
Fiddling on the steps, he buys and sells,
entrepeneurial governor, dual minister,
whose advertising hands hold a straw wreath

Not ecstasy, but anxiety

Fine resolutions adorn self-pity –
What is it he imagines love would solve?
Death's white papers blow through every city
where shadows hawk their blinding charity
from those who saw a talking cure revolve
around a self-delusion full of words
untarnished by thought, of emotion bereft,
like bud-lights dangled to placate the herds
who otherwise might question what rewards
– less an analysis and more a theft.
Anxiety thrives on a high income
its complex childhood skiting its results
and now immune to hurt, instead insults
the legislation it has risen from.

Winter

The Hungarian Church bells ring out
from here to your rich suburb
I walked in like a ghost
generous and bored
away from the scrawling traffic and chipped birds
and listen to the advertising poetry
Below, the green lake like a coin
The streets are full of what I used to know
The music's bladed reeds grow up
I leave where I belong
expecting the Paris Ambassadors
watching another sparkling execution, ironically
It used to be different
but now they come and go the same incoherence
the newest brightest

Real Estates

1

Cheerful Real Estate Agents flash through the apt real estate
their knack and imprecation canvas the roll-up stove
what a jaunt, the doll windows
She turns the ropey key
The application form questions you
on the universe's history

Upstairs they do their nuptials. Here we hold a totally minor
referendum on where to spill and increment
Your Veronica memory holds his Shinto face
that when I saw had urged me to a crown of wit he shucks
in the hardening sun
around the harbour's huge resort

and never see anyone
The corridors finger silently along the numbered doors
her white and turquoise body in the slave walls the drive-in
            temple windows
Six floors down death frills the green pool's vacuous beauty
Lifts jangle or swoop
his slippery violin amongst the brawling TV sets
The stairwell laundered like a garden
Outside gangs of rubbish guard the useful block

2

Across the road from pool the Coronet Fish Markets fade
At home's a dud
Cockroaches huddle on the wall like flowers
He spits his life's lungs through
intermittently like a cigarette
the rattling tunnel of his sleep
that here no odour hides
I spray the poisonous air, his sleep of 'mess and derision'

bald radios play from every room
while on television a leader's doctored face
confronts failure for the last time
He renders to the party and resigns
unguarded finally, the advisers let him fidget or explain

The sizzling oil's surface rucks and webs a stroppy pan
from another flat an old man says 'Don't argue love'
brushing his airless indoor skin
All sleep broken. On sticky walls cockroaches
form dark corsages.
I walk down to the grey timid gentle blades of water
tied boats prick and cross
Junkies deafly march and roll from deal to deal
You can hear each other dream
next door his laddered metal cough
My heart my brain are all locked up

In Perpetuity

1

I spray so nothing's alive
The zigzag carpet feasts
Ponderous sunset settles like a craft
Insects drop and mice weep
Sky's blue saviours comb the lot
Glorious fatal art
whose steeple shames the air
The tin roofs scuttle to the west
You hide behind your feelings
Trams reap past
Matted noise shuffles the flat like cards
and sorrow bores your friends

2

At each death, you go on a bender
In the end, all I can do for you
is wash up and sweep
around your dedicated ash
In death we praised him who life shafted
There's no one left who knows
I go home to broken clocks
Did the public get it wrong
– the glittering personality and failure
when boasts of sorrow fade
The lugubrious conferences continue without you
garnishing the fray
and one by one the marble falls

When I consider

When I consider what my life has been
the tightening streets that stuck me to their side
the turning penitential globe inscribed
with gold and thorn, I picket what I've seen
as if the will were new, the heart were keen
before despair became where you abide
alone with cold ideals and clinging pride
acts and dreams spread out across the screen
I pause at the silky prolonged sunset
that death or god should taper off and shrink
as all the city's woe and all the skies
say not to remember but to forget
and chafing through the cars I fall to think
how sorrows lift and pleasures cauterize

Research

1

It was always dinner then a film
I thought to top it in his public conversation
where it wheeled
Breakfast was a lark, jammed and coincided from the dreams
to fortress like a couple
I couldn't get the hook or when it was
Penultimately I had to blank
Another day to quail, a vice to con for him
Freedom was a drink
as if it killed me
When can I return to where I lived?

2

She polishes her imprimatur
They keel and part as if I were a saint
Coins clack down the ledges. Ships nostalgically turn
I stare into the dribbling rainbow oil spill
conjuring my future
Flames splash the casino. Gentle machines water the streets
Slaves sew my clothes outside the law
I enjoy the government art, visionary and affirming,
and undiagnosed life

Exchange Rates

1

I keep my books in plastic, my heart in the fridge
and don't feel better than people screaming in the street
The Korean violinist plays 'London' Derry Air
I can't read what he gives
For deutschmarks a pile of cut papers
He frowns across the pushing bread
and slips his drinks into a sponge
I wear out my shoes
While you fiddle with numbers
she wins the sincerity comp.
'He never likes me when I'm out
as if I were supposed to be a jug
of assent' the tapping snow
'We love each other but we're incompatible'
she goes, in the bank.

2

Though you wanted to think so, I never was as miserable
You swoon into decline, dying for love
I never feel free enough
Lasers and Toyotas tumble
'Baby talks' 'Cars snarl' the headline swamps
He niggles at me the same for crimes and vices
I visit the countries' smouldering imperialism
the 24 hour conquests, his 'Study of Light' women
Mirrors tunnel in the walls
Answering machines talk across the streets
He shows me his day's itinerary He gives me his crisp card

The playground neon jangles through the night
its tin song of cartoon exchange
Wheels revolve like stars
I never feel myself
We walk around and smile at clothes
The TV drowns. Above the traffic twinkling birds listen

You want to look nice but all you had is gone
and stare into the hot sun's desolation
and shuttle through his intricate solace
coiled like a house. We phone from cell to cell
but clichés ache and sing ardently through the street
to the porcelain gathering

Heroic Money

(2001)

Heroic money

I throw in my lot with them
showing me the crashed lights they drove into
cold isolate Bohemians
My mind is filled with condiments
pompous and self-pitying, which they escape
'I am unworthy'. You bow and leave
and rationalise it by saying it was wrong
Maybe in another world I feast on the detritus
like a business like a hospital
The *Star Trek* editors watch Australiana on TV
the personalities philosophising
Tell the Central Committee we feel bad
lancing the streets
past the brideshops' dulled marbled gleam
It was weather like this when we buried him
drugs and sex cancelling nausea
like it's going out of style
Now the train rides over green palaces of trees
and dribbling oracles

She righteously tails the issue of the week
Here curtained bricks shimmer
Coats of politeness drop each sopping word
I contemplate Autumn behind the rust
sponged red trees flat against mist
like a bandage
Pragmatism makes its corporate entrance
It was good you discovered a galaxy
Goodbye, palindrome,
taxes are close to my heart
Drive behind the Big Events numberplate
where cars jam to the crash or street demonstration
and we wave from our democracy

Oh Anachronism

Oh Anachronism worth preserving
We praise your cylinder engines

Great Feelings have left me
Uplifting nature I don't buy into

We book a place to talk
where I smirk on your behalf

I'd like to not have to stay here, moving in and out
of the cold beach

feeling a landmine with my foot
Couples are the right formation for the ghost-train
sloshing through an echo-tunnel

Your true self has left
the square halo of a living saint

Rameses

Pillar after pillar towers my name
Not all of these could express the life I feel
flash through me
My ideas span the earth

but now tours litter at my feet
folding their waxy guides

Here, I watch life fall apart in front of me
as we hurtle towards death.
I hope you'll last
but every monument freezes

———

My Anatolian agent writes to complain
of my negative review
Words cut me to the bone

I wear what I wore to your wedding
but then the day glittered in sunlight

Tomorrow I'm reading out loud
in services to hedonism
I write my plaque on the spongy world
and hail the puny days

Eurydice's Suburb

1

The wings of home enfold you and lock
under the city's poisoned coronet or halo
You gaze at the supermarket's petrified food
and respond like a zombie to the past's ghosts
and semblance of meaning
Jewelled cigarette, they got on criminally
Sorrow autonomously surges
Affirmations curl up on the fridge

After, we go to the Parthenon Thai restaurant in Northcote
Social workers cleansing their systems on art's scaffold

Each interview an advertisement, relentless song
Noble games sail towards the Equator
with vested interests bidding to the last
or floundering
Conglomerate personality in the Honours list
He calls him by his job
The dollar tilts with raids and hedges

2

Ills and plaudits sift into the ground or flame
when we farewell
Now no one knows your faith a 'spotless lamp'
as mail flaps with ads and tenants come and go
Her stainless presentation scales the house
and Saturday was jokes
velvet streets and the roofs' wedges
sky passes like a film

His distant voice marbles the horizon
Lenten bread or manna falls
robust oasis
I scroll through my life

behind the Valiant Safari and Mitsubishi Executive
They return to their belongings
in pink smog and crowned buildings

3

The city's grids at night, paper lights
tossed in desolate water
in the fish-lined plastic sea
You fall asleep in front of the electrodes
and salute the vacuum-wrapped lunch
The strands of history you concoct, praising the tractor
for its patriotism, you buzz into sunset
having shunned the sea's snapped edge
Great Artist of nostalgia, your overflow cups
bristle with distinction,
your studious oeuvre takes its pulpit
Leaves like words arrange and scatter
and potentates shrug

Portrait of a Man

1

You should've been admiring the brilliant world,
the pouring dictionaries but instead
I pass the men's parliament

At the check-out, he repeats the machine's instructions
which I click, passed to and fro between us
like a precious baby

2

'You should be more conducive
grateful for my chair
What difference will one make anyway?
I know better than to ask'

Machines dribble over the tables, the floor
to failed enterprise
to composts of paper waiting for alchemy
that stink of all you've read

mitre of application, towering reward

3

As the carving renovations at dawn replace the unified subject
unlegislated birds shine in dim afternoon,
each visit an amendment

You asked if you should marry
and then did
but thinking every jibe's at you

I miss what you were being supremely
not an edge, now surrounded by humourless nature
razed landscape like a carpet
and people like windows

The Global Rewards Redemption Centre

1

I heal the ramparts of the deponent tense
I am being loved and certain
A toast to the surgeon's art who cut me
from her skin
the night's software: a drink

I continue my existence as a negative role-model
bathing in the blood of others
sitting in a cone of noise

Birds sing me to sleep at dawn
when you walk in the fabulous cold.

2

across remnants of life
The spiritualist junkies examine their dreams
Nice days pass my window like a train
You follow him into the baptistery or chancellery
a guide for each muted circle
The city's crumbling brocade and souvenir
immortal art
Aluminium pillars shimmer in the bank's foyer
Sail towards the coast
Await the unpassable sorrow

Epilogue

1

His money-making properties come back like a beach
the saintly applications
promoting Australia
Stretched logos bracelet and peck
The Assembly of Experts sits
under exit-coloured roof beams
adumbrated, the brocade trees,
inappropriate, unloved

2

She married her and betrayed him
Faithful knight
Hitched in the car's stifling air
I mope in my truck
World leaders coagulate support
Plough through sugared windows, shops
lilac roses, blue trees
after shining in the shadow of the last government
the heart's melted disk would have forgotten
tanked in the jumbled city
It's summer after the rain
I read the historical novels and the hedge funds wilt

3

Coated in plastic
the newsreader head prefects' amusing formula,
that writes himself off
Extinct species fidget in the wired yard
Later you remember
chained to my clock
Unable to continue I prefer really
Sunset's golden wedge slows the horizon like a door

4

and wear the arrows of your criticism
and empty cup
and wander through the cute waterfall
Enamelled birch tree and broken canvas
Teach me to write
Buildings drift into sky over the reeled sea
and carry the load of separation
and sunset's hinge

Profile

'I started out with a frayed and urgent lyric
I suppose it was a comparative poverty
then learning appealed to me, though the past scared
then the Orpheus poems
a sort of self-commentary
You'll see in my second book how I've
tackled national themes
My spoken word CD
was the people's voice for a while
Later I was avant-garde
You can read the accompanying text's
explication of process

And now, to seem
Priests gather at the table
and swim in the pages of my future
to a world I've barely crept on
The greats I keep at a distance,
fervid for those overlooked by history
to hope perhaps someone attends my book
They crown me with reward'

La Penserosa

Melancholic dandy, you weep and cut
with yearning
Uninterrupted argument, truncated simile
swathed in religion's cold abstract love
The roped bridge's bracelet of light
but shadows cross your face
Paintings slide off into her text, unsolaced
in the porous flat
The past is wagging at your sloth
Responsibilities stagger in a pile
garbled head and licking nightmares
weeping at your wrist
The works don't hang any more
They wallow in their primitive fables,
diligent acolytes
Who pulls me into the world

You'd prefer to not talk
in the ruffled hours
and shut down, away from their distracting company
The private prison opens its cells for business
The corporation welcomes the inquiry
Inside I was panicking
conglomerate regret
and putrid day levitating
Before the rain, birds whistle
as you become a statue
they mate and peck on.

Old Masters

We favour the master bedroom
The galleries' masterpieces, masterfully flourishing
Through the walkman, virtuosi plead
a magna carta of choked respect
Vibrating traffic shillies through night
having mastered its instruments
She slides her mastercard through the scanner, paternally
Patrons show your chair
as master craftsmen wend their way
and the pilot, praying, leaves the cockpit
the manned ship's jilted radar's
one small step...

Success

'No tobacco' she mixes it only with bark and rosebriar leaves
hempened. I turn the sign around
red slash digitalised across a happy throng – 'No Peopling' –
away from my folly
She drinks the soy and yak
demonising the potato
'Turn three times'
and I did, into the pie-shaped future
on the first available
and the jollied drinks her pillar of organza collapses from

The phone clatters shut
Sticking wind winds around the house
She stares 'I got the injections with the pedicure and wax'
self-absorbed like a columnist
The committed tea-towel and toy clothes bang
I take the cake of sadness
Mice slide on dust

His art history peaks to himself
in frozen compass
I search through night cratered
with tumbling dreams and traffic
My Life As An Intersection
whose features thicken
'I knew you once: Leipzig was where.'
Tomorrow's weather fluffs the particles.

Virtue

Guardian of the hearth, trumpeted protocol
She guides the drinks and keys, the jug's tormentor
I address the citizens and go home
Crepuscular music and flattened effect
'a bunch of stuff the death-y bands'
splats over the broken carpet's
model of dissolution
Meteors pound dawn
in an aura of dust mites
Titania and Oberon sing from their paddocks
sonic yodelling, formally naïve
the proselytisers' scrolling sums and fragrant airport
as the pasty weather ebbs

Glorious Mystery

1

When I've finished I'll go out
to the bank's railed glass
spotless, temporary
'The Madonna in a Chair' hangs on plaster
But 'Is God an employer?'
skids through the unreal estates
the wood-panelled hair
Stardust scatters imprisoning music
Bequeathed and betrothed
the twinset couple
hammer in the night
If you want to be breezed on
staggering logo of weather
placebo date
The orthodox establishment abounds
On the left, the cartographers
To our right, the anthropologists are passable
who brio in the refuse dawn
but 'Guilt loves company'
if you take the chaff and bit

2

Engrossed in your subject
I clamour with a thousand people
and stare at the phone's shales
connecting my mesolithic software
Hope no more
borrowed from your spin
I should be more circumspect
reaching for the jab or portion
Where have you gone
counted, forewarned
in the drenched music, petrified subject,
where I swot virtue in the glimmering streets
carrying my dull encyclopaedia
and the report's burden

Paganini

'I'm tired and I loathe travelling
Achilles is my consolation
He comforts me with unspeakable affection
Cold Britons, I fulfilled your desire for something new
You filled my pockets and we are quits'
The new futility follows me abroad
Puffed wedding of nostalgia and amnesia
The old hits tap the floor
I scour Paris in theatre of this mime
Europe wrangles, ascending mediocrity
leering at my bliss
Nothing staves the draught that ticks me

Ode to Trouble

1

Before tea I play Mozart on the violin
After, I walk my estate
Platonic friends I think of you often
when ascending the meaningless stairs and hitched portico
and my faithful slave hums death
to greet the worthy city
beneath the mink and ermine, the solipsist wedding
Veiled empire my calculus is bad
I wrote a gloss on days
gulched heap or mound
as still as sleep
The arsenic pitched in
You're outside the zone of observance
neither science
Correct hard-hearted friends
He wants to be like the sermon on the
and not a newsreader, carrying truth's water-pistol

2

'I felt that I was getting somewhere with my work
hardening like wax and holding me
but priorities change. I rub his wordless back
I mean we're carbon'
and wake up on the nightmare's edge and spruce
as roaring day and phoneless night distribute your effects
but only work sings any kind
its pontoon of remembrance, I get across

Mary Wollstonecraft

1

'Now the teachers bore me
He passes, with his fallen interests
preaching what benefits, softened tyrant
He talks over my life
like a plane overhead
a different current
I thought I was fated but I was not
Drenched river'
Stranger to doubt, she splashes
'The fat ex tussling his portfolio beseeched whispers
Garments sink
and failure washed away
He unloves me'

2

'Sister I took from him
but languished governess...

Now I thread hands through sea
on this rocked shore, and flag your business
as food clips and fearful maid scratches
Your child also hecks and ails
Torrents block us and the awning water and silence knifes'
She writes in a feast

3

'We found more sure
our time spilled together
who could not know this last
I leave you what's living, loved and better,
though the changed doctors undo'
and arrow freezes

Swoons

She tells of her swoons
many and varied, smitten and occult
and then the wholesome novelist's parents appear, endearingly
and play their squeamish assessment
Green necklace, the sad viola focuses
Drums accompany the shot of the window

You look the future in the artery
You look love in the foot
enjoying the emptiness
as the no-story play's women skeet and blip
The meaning of her song, frayed and timely,
slats through the personality's dull work
in a sorority of fame

How should I capture the blue newspapers
the hanging cords

Malvolio

I dress up and swish, imagining you turn
having rumoured and harried the poles of trees, the straitened
      avenues
that dream your words like logs binding into me
gentle and parsimonious
I fish what could woo
from my printed books
as formerly assail,
what favoured words, clouds oil sky
and green tiles pan the orange brick walls'
school windows and silent factory
where you walk, unpatched
enjoying the view and the attached sorrow
The stars screwed and books topple
I retrieve a glowing notice, a ghost invite, that treachery compresses
to your sphere and voice of accomplishment and starlit do

Dignitaries

1

Light abides and hailing trees
comb the house's pinched list
gradually cancelling all that you need, the tap
drips and weeds weave
and the factory's roof plates your window
Factory birds pipe like an alarm

2

She's doing the *mastering*
Dust mauve light treacles across the floor
in their expressive house
His voice sits like gladwrap, favoured servant
Bored by the men's music
I'm so into not having a car
and find you in my dreams
my talisman, my completion
budding through years

3

The father beats his wife and kids, but basically
a good bloke and by the end loveable
The film's patriarch chant
Counselling the murder victims
here in Ekaterinberg, the main highway
for top-grade heroin,
I've had a great hit,
That's Thursday, 8.30
Night plucked from its box
Receipts dangle, the coiled phone snaps
Reassess the opening gift, the gaffe

4

I cut him when my eggs halved
Now I rub preservatives into my books and skin
Curiously satisfied with life's bricks
I inject my heart to enter your city
'And light is thy fame'
The household junkie puffs her libation to the keyless tenant
It was time out but hammed

5

Proust's decorated parents he says, interviewed
Ten pages of the unassuming novelist
Coldness beseeches the window's logs
Irreconciled CD
dreams running and screaming

Unused to how to, couples knock like boughs, stretched tryst
or the sorrow of, ladled
and dunced words you puzzle like a friend

6

Grey clouds scrap through wire
and last birds call
The factory's instruments click and saw
Industry bangs shut like a bell
and belief pricks the footpath into shards of past moments

7

Our leader says *sophistry*, as in no amount of
Money and sundries spill out of the couch
Screened goody comedians spar a charm of ignorance
In the silent world, day draws
its curtained doubts in the iced street
a coupled and/or babied populace stroll
as rooms full of words slump like jewels
a cesspit, a binary set
Sometimes the ghost of the street comes to you
like a stockcube
He loves her to stop her

Cosima Wagner's Book of the Dead

He gives me the pen he wrote with,
the hair from his eyebrows.
The sublime music welcomes me on the stairs.
My transcendental love wishes death,
sublime heroism. I wash his clothes.
Ivy covers his tomb. He gives me *Eau de Richard*.
I look for his creations in my face, his hands to make me.
For you, I've soundproofed the house in felt.
I suffer to myself while he flocks.
Dramatic adjunct, I take my palfrey and ride
to relinquish all genetic traits
and promise to live better.

Actaeon

I took them racing in the lime fast air
to hunt and run and kill
their prey, the lesser forms of old despair
in thrall to nature's spill
A copse of shade to catch my breath
a fish packed pool
parting in a ring
when gold flesh
rises and withdraws
then eyes catch out and echo wrath
my career, my dogs who tear
my limbs, a stolen flute
falls in the seeping grass

Thelma's Hamlet

1

But now his boated smiles like a brother...
She glues through the shops' bare gift and drapes
Why decorate this wreck?
arch caught in a pillar
not like it used to be
He descends inside bright imagination
serving persuasively
Harness another day's tightening windows
whose patched blind whose watched screen
So not surprised having extinguished
those nearest and. Rivals gather like cavalry
trying to knock from her
Food's out of the way
but new drugs, slavish and excellent, scale and not covet
What stencilled plume rises above her head
to sincerely dub those fortunate
to pass or rock the players' sickled tears

2

Under the suburb's Dutch sky
the freeway's lake
Drive towards the flag
on its slate-squared tower

but fawn night glides
and past work like embossed plasticine
cyphers and falls, scattered dolls
It's one big moomba
On speaking terms, bereft and ultimate
Keep your flogged programme
and nagged ghost
The roué's charmed life ends
and then nothing.
say the drive-in flowers
        and books.

Fallen Athlete

Admiring the neighbour's nutritious garden
and subdivisions of time, you eat dinner from a jar
and work and play referring to an ivory abacus
Your head emptied of levity looks to the topaz horizon
as you wash past the crate houses and slept-in clothes
and compromised landscape
to scrape art from the lot. Or reach for less in the end
pushing aside the tulips and populism
hitched by the cheering rally whose tears cross the view
Shadows stretch the field, exhausted at every step
The stadium's golden track's wound like a spring
Liquid day flees past, dappled and quick
and limbs a sheet
The sun crossing ahead and the loosened harbour's
plough and practice
You fall into yourself and nothing, whistling like grass

Pushkin

The court jealousies and intrigues where I tarnish
blunt and bored where her glitter is a shower
At the estate, nothing comes
She shines, a caller
and now her minions wish
Tedium and convention where life flutters out
amused at a distance
but books trail with sums and bombast passes
On the coldest day, your horses slip
to the outskirts where errors fall,
but I had wished it ended
Inexorable snow, I push from her and pardon
'Goodbye, my books'
(and dies)

Electra to Clytemnestra

Your jewels and cut and my chopped dress
and awkward husband
in the lounge where he slinks
in a puff of
Hansel and Gretel jump from the idling ute
Sliced moon, you frolic
and robes sass my dirt floor
while I tear my hair, my brother's footprints chip
and old flowers drop as you crony
through pamphlets of behaviour
for your blow-in – old admirer in his hushed shirt
proffering a bar stool while my herd goats bleat

Aztec'd life of laurels and libations
who died in the cause
I texta out stains and mistakes on my clothes
and pan the earth for ribboned hope
apart, a clue, his grassy voice cracked like an axe
or false memory that shoos you to a bride
A king at work a cairn at home
when night clumps like a jigsaw
You choose the finish and intent in your spiralled city's
claimed suburb where I'm hostage to your incursions
your whim to broach my brother's track
his beauty has left me that used to crinkle air. I tramp through ash
to look for the most wished for

Ismene to Antigone

You should talk some sense into his head
and not stick by, constant samovar
Do you also look for the one love
Good deeds, selfless and arcane
and soulful breakfast. Your crisp assault
to flout and ally the tampered roof that kept us,
a glacier of blood, if your catafalque progresses and the keeners ring
past the sunbleached shops' archived ads and forked clothes
and each branded corner and cloud
The mountain shone with neon
above the stacked electric wires toning your street
but I grind into the work
that words might peel his heart
Remember how they fell who went before

New Poems

The last Spring

1

The last Spring scents Chekhov's verandah where we yarn
But you were sad before
Another moon's come and gone
unloved cartel of lines and bones
Drugs dissuade her as she hoovers the streets
in broken day's enforced idleness
that music snipped like wings
and her mauve assistant
You sympathetically die
as the sky's navy river tips
over the car-light stars

2

Magpies sing late morning
through the neighbours' concern

while, anaesthetised,
you watch fish-scales glint on the peace-talker's lips
her talc'd hands sit aloft
and sleep like your cat

'Overseas markets' splits the drama series
Your hands, my hands
Your skin, my skin
The sun comes up like serial murder
You take on the mantle of authority that dies
through the ghost trees' column

3

In the museum
past loves fade on the wall
squinting at your own reflection
Another statue felled in the rock-white garden

So death comes, with his scythe and his spade
his looped television

———

The mynah bird calls out
Don't leave me
alone in this world
The edifice crumbles
Red sun logos Sudafed on the shy horizon

———

Have a joint before his chemo
at white-wheeled dawn
on a litter of cigarettes

and drive through the suburbs
as Syd King and his Five Strings play

4

Lined palm trees cone the orange water
We meet at the spectacular
where fireworks cling to black sky
Pessimism hangs in your wallet like an address
your tin of foreign coins
and mobile picasso, loved sphinx
I held last year in my hand
Artesian belvedere of memory
Tomorrow, you get laminated
I went to Antarctica to learn about myself
The grief counsellors were rushed to the scene

Travel

Birds waver and spear through the hotel window
Trees majestic and brushed
in the streets of Morocco
or the plains of Troy
If you gave me a mountain
His faded hands throw the poems away
The great trees flick in the courtyard
and shallow tram tracks mossed
Snowing fir tree, laced with dust
Broken flowers
in the airport's smoked limbo
You stick with those you hurt
His fuchsia dress, empanelled and cohesive
inert as a stump
Dollar-obsessed pragmatist
baking in your landscaped garden
You kiss the cigarette's fund
Greetings in Dutch

City

A week ago you were a different person
Now soaring art sours
He works through his machines, digitalising your words
Anodised ring
we embark on normality

and protest from the glove box
of your brother's caprice
lollied trees and mountainous buildings
He's lined against the drinks
Make it a double I'll join my friends sooner
Addiction in the recycle bin
when you have to leave the cities of nostalgia

Priam

I drop the warrior shield
these undone greaves
Puzzled ant on the footpath
or pet window-sill spider
sings out in its endurance
I come mechanically propelled and halting
between the shore and the citadel
to your stretched tent's garlands of triumph
as the sheet blows from you
I poach and lag
a living pyre
Just an ounce of time would get me what I want
and drop on the wet hands that killed him

Cracked Avenues

Ismene

You live in the cracked avenues
arguing and warming a kitchen's generations
Last year wept but now the harrowed road

Moths eat the library, huffing past
The best went flickering through folding birch and sycamore
Last year was but now the bladed veil

Once sunset chipped in your hair, farewelling the universe's
          inhabitants
Now clouds stop in your frozen cemetery
your wine-dark car turning in the drive
Advertisement flags serrate the 7-Eleven's pediment, the streetlights
          set like spoons
Graves dust the hill and the ruptured gums
that whistle your instructions

   ——

You take the opal moon for granted
the marching cypress, sunset's bolt
the street's green strip neon selling food
at every calamitous funeral red car lights map like lava
Gold kalashnikov's meted sorrow, an orb, a card

   ——

New Year's Day shines on next door's brick wall and chimney
as photos turn the marvellous gardens' First Communion
writing your doctorate on the pillow
whose chains and sigh have passed
I pull the hearth rug's Martha and Mary into my caul

149

A golden hypocrite reassembles in the Arch of Federation
You, who were always with me, remember how bright the stars
above the ti-tree and eucalypt

We sat out in the fallen landscape, severed from what was
colouring the yard as it had been
She says you're running now in the gold paddocks of your youth
who never reached her age
We lay the falcon china
Above, the hilted Southern Cross

———

Antigone

They take away from me what they inspire
He went to what he was
For so long I represent you, a cachet
of just and true, that bones walk instead
and have to rebuild brick by brick
glorious atlas and swab, the stars, the shark sea satin'd
to become what you satirise
back to the circus and caravan
Weepy avenger coarse ground doesn't touch
– clang of sword on mattress –
I hold your fake hand to my brow
to feel love turn on and off like a programme
illustrating a cliché

———

Blogs fugue into themselves,
stripping time across the shuttling lists
as music plaques over a sacked diary
and the egghead blurb's mountain of claims
and heroic tasks depicted on your shield
You know it like a bath of dirty water
How did you get stuck in that tide of boasts

and souvenirs, his royal eyes light
on the past's porphyried gas
having chucked the dolls of irony
in childhood's plastic bushes and lain path
who slab the air, obstinately
Illness drags you to the talkshows of resolve and parried death
a maypole streamers reach to, a cabinet of poison
that twins each other in dispensation for the chute

You breach the galleries' biblical catalogue and pyramid of sand
A tinker of song fulfils the relationship you meant to cut
trimmed and cobbled, sworn in on a whim
Rain snaps into place for myself but you, unmourned
who prepared bitterly
Thumbing a mobile, I turn from the choir

———

Kangaroo and Emu

1

He surveys the tilled electorate, covets
his faded abacus of watched commentators
hauled jockeys who don't know what's missed
The record leader gnaws his record to the core
family smote around him in a lei
'We stick with what we know'
says the marginalled, marshalling her TV bytes
a bodyguard of season's values and the stressed deputy
tiddlywink attentively

2

'Excitement for the first time in yonks' a struck gallery keys
as the new leader estimates the stage
His kids circuit the maths chairs
An ex sighs

Aspirations whine like a semaphore
when popularity slated its
gift selves from the Tree of...

'We have signed niiine memoranda' the minister umpteenths out
ramping up his slush fund's rumpled horn
or promise to change Tuesday to Monday
pulling a lizard from a hat
a ring of certainty buttered on his finger
raffling through a sulk, a ute
a nodule sheared off by his mates

3

Swaggering misanthrope marooned in a nib
you go through the liege bracelet
and plethora friends living in their own coinages and scam

   'We decide who comes into this country'
   by algorithm or parachute
   'and the circumstances in which they come'

with always the assumption that anywhere is better
crimson paddock and peppercorn or clattered heath he can't beguile
a punter of woe riding out of luck.

Sister to memory

Time contemplates your splendour
and realm of certitude
before rain closes the sky
She texts me of her woe and debt
in the assisted wonderland
My superlative, my hypocrite
Cool parents at the swings and kids upright
A line of clothes ballets in the breeze selling or drying
Architecture slumps and soft furnishings shoulder the riddle,
          the street
and faxed emotions
Once Beethoven seeped in the floor we lay's dated theology
Now art freezes in your hands
the lobbed day's pell of sums and blue accounts
Search through the library of old taxes
Always the day's switched on, her scarfed headphones
and the strobed button undoing conversation
life removed from itself, google the answering universe
that observations clot in your head

The swimmer retires

While I read through the old records
the city builds outside. There's no texture
to the stale ribbon. Medals press on your casket
Over winter, I swam through each brief dawn
polish the useless talent
in the carved water
All honours wash away
> *He falls through the mist of reporters*
> *veered from a dream*
> *– a jewelled car that magnets round a coast*

The pool unsheathed from me
The lanes unlock
as tallied seconds clang out each rubbed line
The hand on heart's forgotten anthem
and splashed cameras
> *He turns from the blue aisles*
> *A king a servant thankfully going*

Tormented syllogism held at bay

Each day you remember an entire life
festooned with silence, enthralled by a tree
and walk back into the legend of the beach's
zipped water and bucking dolphins
Another predecessor's dug up
a cheese-grater in its heyday
another meteor shower
Plastic sacks hang like scales
and websites tick into the aether
polling your consumption or pity

The interrupted CD's broken aerial
makes you try surprise
old Maroochydore of the mind
bumped up with the available
as when the cherried sky falls behind the dishes
jutting a wagging finger
a wind-up statuette of pure intention
perfecting the art of the suburbs
through the pale supermarket's aisles

Or drive into the intersection's law that no one follows
out of one life into another
automatic roads and washed rhododendron
wails the redemption song
whose 'hearts are out of order'
that Pyramus and Thisbe scat
Crayon elm and stitched grass sink for you,
and planes open the canned estates
printed on a ridge

She folds her hard-earned into a platypus
– a market for your thoughts – and reassures his elbow
A proscenium of other lives ascends into the heavens
Bright star I wish I were as remote and singular
sparkling in the debris and not a mash
Ships slip the horizon
and unharmed novelists walk home in leaking sun
She dusts herself off and keels over in a binge
She was the ones she loved
Farewell youthful carousers most unwritten
Remember sea beneath the gulls, now clouds nod in the buildings
and Goth Estate Agents twirl the rivet keys

The Constant Measure

The oven's tipped open as a bar heater
its red art deco zags another age's
faith in a designed century
as a Chevrolet unscrolls up the hill
and the painted-from-life steeple's
pleated shadows carve out long wedges
specifying a theorem you once knew, like your life,
sparkling over the top of a drink 'Spirit of the Plains', etc,
while every unwinding gesture
salutes some mirage or schtick tilting on its axis.

The landscape doesn't change. The tree collects its rings
Hope's waterlilies bubble on the pond's face
accompanying imagination that conjures his blank escarpment
but softness fields, by leaf and fork,
its pained accoutrements offer a silenced fee,
betrayed either way.

It's full-time being pluralist
Days tolerably mashed at each step in glorious streets
At home wind foots the skating glass, crooked lintel,
soundless pages. Water botched upon the fern.
Anyone can paint it.

Memoir's First Premiss

If only it were then whose filed brain you stow and restore
the one for crying
where sun and shade cross a dreamt cheek
as air disconnects ferried clouds humming overhead
and earth wheels from sun
that frits last locked above the treetops and waxed roads

At the txt you throw a u-turn via mutability
while dual captains sail into cooked sunset and tender isthmus
happy see anti-depressants
and the second form of lyricism enters on castors
hallowing its blog

while the video rolls
on kids scrunching up the forever water
but that's the past cooeeing from a bluff
Now plastic sequins the country
and the ghosts of everyone come

Oppenheimer at the Un-American Activities Committee

Their questions began, then suppositions, then hypotheses
Each angle parried, pushed. At first, my answers tripped,
nicely true, but as the hours, the weeks arranged
around me – a *case* – sure that I could see the slip,
of course corrected and jotted, helpful, when applicable, to make precise
the day, the set, the score. The rote I knew
each angeled formula stringed in air, canyon-neat
yet they still wheedled, wondered if, what meeting meant
and my students, co-workers, rise above that gashed and made horizon
        that we summed
and friends turn who tended, a whistling parade
they shuffle and chalk my 'defects in character'
and then a morsel, a speculation, creaks. *I have so little self remaining*
and crisp till then *I am*... and recollection folds and what I was too

Western Isles

Stretched like a tarpaulin, courting moments
hooded Unabombers fold clothes in the laundromat
as their nacreous fleeces twirl
and twilight tumbles over date-less posters:
charities and cars,
last year's parish fête's handwritten yearning
Air force manoeuvres have shorn the TV
from its porridge of comfort's renaissance colours
Measly rain tars straight roads that thither
as real estate cools to your bank statements

Gibbering at the floral table's hems
poisons join you to the world
Scottish hornpipes play at the funeral of happiness
through books of ticking time
Another loss files into the ground
that art laments

That laments

You want to live as far away as possible
from those diamond casts and footnotes
that used to have the confidence of ten

welcoming strangers
Now, she never wants to crush
steam rising from her feet like a future

You pass the tomb of the Unknown Poet
remorseless and dedicated
scared that words might fall out on the drive

waiting for some witticism to chap the cups
Now he makes a puppet of himself
who loved it *as an artist*

and, *as a parent*, was taxed to very height
Papers nap over the watching clips,
dandling as career,
they go home to the aether in a lake.

Ascension

1

Guardian bugs and clarinets screw air
where flowers pop in berated streets, the local Erechtheion
at ease among hoarse dogs and tiptoe possum
At sunset floodlights crown the valley
beneath the freeway and pushed stars
a biding desk
that night flanges and czar camellias
talc the church ground, the country on a hill
whose windows pine your former names
nuggeting the pastures but chiefly, stacks.

Thermos the inspirations and curtsied pasts'
emollient regions
here under the Moreton Bays and data

2

that slam you back from there
to your *sole self* – or is it
She masquerades the suburb unto death
and recalls the mystic's abandoned child's
a wilting thorn in his ascent

Bookbinding a seethed alignment you taxi into
or embody
Old jokes enamelled on a cornice
over a tiled wall furnaced
up to heaven and vanish coldly

Savonarola

Cheerily inquiring, I came to Heaven's gate open to a simple throne,
the sky perforated with stars
and Jupiter's two-faced moon trailing its orbit
'Teach my walking soul'

A power station's lights and racetrack's beams
pompom the hill and flick along venetians like notes on a stave
Rain pills the screens and art's gaudy stanzas
as I read, the introvert's cable, or Arno, takes me

Shirker of my class, gratuities slither off
like a magisterial chain,
blotting the ink on *An Urchin's Guide to Domesticity*
but rue besieged me

They come to hear him talk of art
and flock to the Sadness Panel alleviated and wronged,
a maimed tent fits the news, plumed mountebanks
spruiked from a cypress

Nothing superfluous. We decked our clothes in sack,
speckled books and garbed painting,
fervent Weepers admonishing a rose
while a crane's brand-name tiaras night

Three mount a cross, but first they hanged my friends
air scooped out from under, the placard square
I follow where I preached
hanged then burned over my 'privileges'

wanting to dis-embroider all their ilk and paste
crocheting dinner, flirting on a tithe.
and drop.
The Pope commissions a new architect.

Echo

Another all-night slugs through their scammed oeuvre
that critics nimbled in a water-taxi
but thanks for the extirpation I sift into my panniers
and ride the new estate's jellied hills
meanwhile advertising
Brokered trees mush fields
and a blind's fronds of green twilight
raft over the bed and baffled cat piloting a thesis on itself
Revolving doors tie behind you in a sash
Put the garden in a drawer that sniffed memory's mopped obeisance,
now a few rooms testify
and his hands krill the glassy pool

Stuck in Traffic

She meant it was good to yarn, no trauma
Now you get how you mistook
swotted totally at the braked drinks and slipped physics, you're over

She's bumping in for the show and doesn't deign to risk
a charge or block, and her child 'suffers absence'
Four churches sharpen the intersection

You know what? I cancelled, it wasn't cogito precisely
but who could've, like I put it out there
my sessions and criteria all one-on-one a tray

across a bridge's attempt at grace
while ads strew the transport's view
into meshed ideograms of capitalism

I jibbed into a cube, shonky life blinking through a glass, a pick,
then hoiked what's left of friends.
It's of no purpose.

I don't want to see him a radish or leek.
Chimes pester down what boredom spored
and goes, a meddler to the heath

You buy the lock for the door then the door for the lock
as cords corolla sealed ears that hyphen thought
to home in the electric fields

Parting Winter

Twinned letters, formal as nothing now is,
the flight napkins sewn with sums, statistics, possibilities

over the pointed seas, 'the cost of ambition'
Skelter your lives

near the steaming University
or paved in wedding snaps, his cut suit, her belled satin

'Even just a glimpse of your handwriting would be enough'
Research papers feather in the mill's craw

'No idle chat', 'less time off'
Orchids and lilies fall from your veil

'When will I make amends?'

The house snips shut
Now a pool-blue sky turns to frost
and years you never see cast over

Iphigenia

Ships slinged in low elastic waters knock
who chug you to the altar
where old blood crumbles.
Orange fire tassels air.
You look out from the coast

back when twisting horses rise...
and clay figurines scout on your shelves
or back, lost geraniums shimmered August
and then expunge, then 'fluey tenants later, then tied between two
        screens
your binary presence more real than soft dawn
when ritual tatters
and reversible names converse over the galloping maps.

Her teary pillar shrives a velour sea.
Your hair tacked with daphne and myrtle. Birds creak, a charmer –
nett bridegroom, mock stag –
to keeling ships, to dimple wind
coins close your eyes

The Marriage of Arnolfini

Jan van Eyck, 1434

On the sill an apple signifies the fall,
her gleamed face twines over the future
who slots and turns
There was no hope of understanding
Still he stands in funeral dress
She is what might have been
An altercation in the yard diverts
His outdoor shoes chucked
Bring the vigil candle
breaths tumbled into day
Rank and broom hang behind in pact
but light melts to the wick

Aeneas

I carry you across, away from the burning citadel
away from a life eluding resolution

carrying nothing on your back
crossing the water

and prefer the pinging emptiness
as yesterday's baubles clout the anvil and squirt regret

Husbands top your drink
A tureen of alternative lives spills from the waiter's grasp

I chew a fife and play
and sovereigns weep

Tchaikovsky in Italy

Every passing carriage drives me mad
Every shout, every sound, lacerates my nerves

as he gives out what used to attract
Each year a new thing hated

though you loved the town's forgotten gang
Free at last to lack at leisure

as glee recalls its vast paddling pool
Emoticon of happiness shins down a skylight

and cheeping quartets wafer to an urn
Dismiss your foes, of which many

over clopped seas, blame follows
its pressed blue wedding roses

skiffle my return

Daphnis and Chloe

He rides a segway through the topiaried hedges
of the *Institut pour le Développement Harmonique*
Next it's granite and a TV spin-off
while she squirms in the scullery, an emulsifier
and a theodolite on each hand
when in Preston she crossed a ditch of sobs

She gathers the covenant to heart, before it lobs
her followers. Thought sledges
a wicket, but whether from glee or a stand
against corruption, who knows, a fit of pique
may as well summarise. She blogs: a death-defier
He pails water from a trough

parting a fence's palings with finesse, a cough
whistles. The demonstration magnifies her probs
and immanence, an astrolabe warped like a tyre
falls across some scratched ledgers
that yearn to annotate and squeak
of her chlorophyll, but awfully fanned

cards gloat and claim the land
was swamp. All bets are off
Return to the campfire: its clique
substitutes logs for chairs and sprigs for knobs
a saddle supporting her head edges
its cinders, i.e. the remains of a local flyer

promoting the environment, as if what they require
could ever class a gluey saraband
over dinner of fried wedges
He resumes the inspection, with Prof.
at an elbow, advising how to maximise jobs
and measuring exactly where the fountains leak

Whirr of helicopter off screen, over to Seek
.com. Either that or the National Choir
warbling probity, while an overseer dobs
her in. His wistful Peter Pan'd
check a rabbit fence will slough
the paddocks, while sunset's pink valve ceases pledges

– all Greek to her, she dredges
up some prior ownership, he bobs
among the damned, all the usual stuff

Ethel's Lethe

1

You looked out, lost throne,
as I pushed you through the native gardens
Birds flew by us, and time past them
my sanctuary and commitment
The city that you'd loved was Autumn
that fêtes the streets with gold
your last voices falling through years
over England's snow the daffodils blushed out
among the fireworks when your diaries end

Now midnight's faint prayers slice into the room and freeze
the bright world going
and breaths stop air
and all love leaves

2

Fog hushes the road over the river,
mossy drive, bustled kitchen, panelled halls
that in the end were clung to
Shadows press the wire door you've left
Hostess to fortune, throw out her crystal dresses
I reach to where she was
Chords kiss skinned time and 'empowering' ads
Another flat turns down an application like a bed

Streets tot surveillance, planes chortle
as you slip on the party's patois, *I'd never seen so much mould*
he says, mouldless and flawless, even in the drooped lights and
          astro turf,
some corker
we brace the past behind, treadling through stern portraits
to chance a dill and friend a ghost who greets
We climb aboard. Decades swatch open.

Southern Aurora

You have to unclip the world to think it
from cloyed screen or scream words haste
their loot and return to her/his sleep-out
sucking troth's lozenge
as the film waves magnolia
on brushed sky childhood seams
and a tinny cafe's wine plaits the house languages and Euro-pop

> *When they marvelled to a reel, an air,*
> *the golden wheat was made of us*
> Now ghost cats come tinkling over grass
> who reigned fearlessly,
> locked in death
> They rise and track the stars

night mutes
while you watch another country's 'lap of pain' win,
his face bevelled in the anthem
Here cars sopped and rain was out of kilter
Time moves further away from you
Memory stifled the jonquils
and you're in a tube of dreams, swimming

NOTES

Forfeit (78): 'appointed to tribulation' (1 Thessalonians 3.3); 'affliction is the way', Søren Kierkegaard, *Edifying Discourses: A Selection*.

Paganini (129): quotes from letters of Paganini, Jon Rose, *Paganini's Last Testimony*, The Listening Room, ABC-FM radio.

Thelma's Hamlet (138): Moomba is an annual Melbourne festival.

Kangaroo and Emu (152): The Tree of Knowledge, Barcaldine, Queensland where the Australian Labor Party was founded during the Shearers' Strike in 1891; quotes from Australian Prime Minister John Howard, 2001.

Tormented syllogism held at bay (156): 'Our hearts are out of order', *Andy's Gone With Cattle*, Henry Lawson.

ACKNOWLEDGEMENTS

Grateful acknowledgement is made to the editors and publishers of the books in which these poems previously appeared, particularly Robert Adamson and Veronica Sumegi for permission to republish poems from *Pure and Applied* (Paper Bark Press, 1998) and *Heroic Money* (Brandl & Schlesinger, 2001). Earlier poems are reprinted from *The Division of Anger* (Transit Press, 1981), *Manners of an Astronaut* (Hale & Iremonger, 1984), *The Last Interior* (Scripsi Publications, 1986), *Excavation* (PanPicador Australia, 1990) and *Research* (Folio/Salt, 1998). New poems in this book have appeared in *The Drunken Boat, Ardent Sun, Best Australian Poems 2003, 2007, 2009, 2010, 2011, HEAT, Jacket, The Warwick Review, Alhambra Poetry Calendar, Southerly, VLAK*.